Group process for nurses

MAXINE E. LOOMIS, R.N., Ph.D.

Professor of Nursing, University of Michigan School of Nursing, Ann Arbor, Michigan

Illustrated

THE C. V. MOSBY COMPANY

St. Louis • Toronto • London   1979

The C. V. Mosby Company
11830 Westline Industrial Drive, St. Louis, Missouri 63141

Library of Congress Cataloging in Publication Data

Loomis, Maxine E
    Group process for nurses.

    Bibliography: p.
    Includes index.
    1. Nursing—Social aspects. 2. Small groups.
I. Title. [DNLM: 1. Group processes—Nursing texts.
2. Leadership—Nursing texts. WY105 L863g]
RT86.5.L66   301.18'5'024613   78-31261
ISBN 0-8016-3037-1

GW/M/M 9 8 7 6 5 4 3 2 1   02/B/217

Group process for nurses

Preface

Small groups are naturally occurring phenomena within the life experiences of clients and nurses. Like most people, they usually belong to a work group that requires that they communicate and solve problems together to accomplish their work objectives. They may also belong to a friendship group that interacts less formally but that has some clear behavioral expectations of its members and anticipates that being together will be both fun and supportive. Depending on their life circumstances, the client and the nurse may also belong to various task-oriented groups such as a church choir or a committee within the district nurses' association. The members of these groups may have secondary social reasons for participating, but the primary group goal or purpose for coming together is usually clearly stated.

The purpose for presenting small group content in this book is to provide nurses with information that will assist them in meeting the psychosocial health care needs of clients. Because I have drawn upon theory from group dynamics research as well as group treatment literature, much of what will be presented may sound very similar to the group dynamics that occur naturally in the environments of the clients and nurses. In fact, the reader is encouraged to draw upon life experiences that may help to explain and clarify the group phenomena being examined. The overall objective of this book, however, is to provide nurses with assessment, intervention, and evaluation tools that will assist them in utilizing small groups to therapeutic advantage in meeting the biopsychosocial health care needs of clients.

Four interdependent variables are examined in *Group Process for Nurses*. Section I presents small group objectives and discusses the advantages and disadvantages of using groups as a vehicle for delivering psycho-social health care. Group objectives cannot be discussed in isolation from group structure, process, and outcomes; therefore, an overview of these variables is presented to assist the reader in assessing small group objectives. This section also includes a schema for categorizing the various types of therapeutic groups that are available to clients.

The discussion of small group structure in Section II provides guidelines for developing and structuring group experiences to assist in the restoration, maintenance, or improvement of the psychosocial functioning of clients. The nurse's interventions related to small group structure include client selection, responsibilities of the leader for physical arrangements, preparation and protection of clients, and clarification of group treatment contracts.

Section III, on small group process, deals with the intricacies of leader-ship roles, interaction of members, and use of various curative factors once the group is in progress. Different types of groups are followed as they deal with initial concerns, the development of group cohesiveness, the working phase of group life, and termination issues. Special emphasis is placed on the development of group cohesiveness, because it has such an impact on the overall functioning of the group. Termination in groups merits a chapter of its own, because it is so often ignored as a significant event in the life cycle of small groups.

Finally, Section IV, on small group outcomes, explores the maintenance, learning, and behavior change outcomes that can result from the group experience of clients. Various measures to evaluate client outcomes and therapeutic effectiveness are presented along with ideas for the future research of health care groups.

The theory presented in this book has been selected for its usefulness in explaining and altering the client's biopsychosocial situation. Special atten-tion has been given to the unique role of the nurse in assisting clients to deal with alterations in their biopsychosocial functioning. Nurses are viewed as health professionals capable of providing clients with integrated health care and teaching that will promote, maintain, and restore their optimum state of functioning.

Regarding nursing interventions that utilize small groups as a medium for the delivery of nursing care, I expect that nurses will function as group leaders. The labels of teacher, leader, facilitator, and therapist are all used in this book to refer to the health professional who assumes leadership and treatment responsibility for the objectives, structure, process, and outcomes of the group. The difference in terminology refers to the uniqueness of the role and not to the professional background of the person who occupies it. A nurse with the appropriate education, supervision, and experience can occupy each of these roles; this issue is addressed throughout.

I would like to acknowledge the contributions of the numerous clients, students, and professional colleagues who have participated in my growth and development as a group leader. I trust that we have all learned and benefited from our involvement with each other in the process of change.

Maxine E. Loomis

Contents

ix

Section IV

Evaluation—
small group outcomes

Group process for nurses

Section I

Assessment— small group objectives

A group is a collection of individuals who are to some degree interdependent. Within this definition, a number of people waiting for the elevator do not constitute a group. If that same collection of individuals needs to decide whether or not they will allow smoking on the elevator, then they become a group for the purpose of making that decision. Their common task has made them interdependent and, therefore, a group.

Research on the dynamics and impact of small groups has increased in the United States since World War II. Sparked by the classic studies of Kurt Lewin and his colleagues, the discipline of social psychology was born and gradually began uncovering answers to numerous questions of social influence and attitude change. In one of Lewin's studies,[1] he explored methods of changing attitudes toward foods. By obtaining commitment from housewives in a group teaching setting, he was able to persuade them to increase their family's intake of readily available organ meats such as brains and kidneys.

In another early study, White and Lippitt[2] explored the effects of leadership behavior and the "social climate" of the group on the behavior and productivity of group members. They developed a methodology for examining the behavior of individuals and groups, and their results demonstrated some clear differences among the effects of authoritarian, democratic, and laissez-faire leadership.

In a parallel line of development, group psychotherapy emerged on the treatment scene in the 1920s and 1930s. Psychiatrists and psychologists of varying theoretical backgrounds—Freudian, Sullivanian, Rogerian—be-

1

gan exploring the application of their treatment frameworks to groups of patients. During World War II, group psychotherapy was used in the military because of the large number of patients and the relatively small number of psychiatrists available to treat them. The effectiveness and economy of treating psychiatric patients in groups gradually led to the integration of group psychotherapy into the education and practice of psychiatric clinicians, nurses, psychiatrists, psychologists, and social workers.

It was not until the 1960s that group dynamics and group psychotherapy actually converged. That decade saw an almost unprecedented growth in the area of interpersonal relations and personal awareness, now referred to as the encounter group movement. The sharp lines of demarcation between T-groups (training groups), sensitivity groups, therapy groups, and encounter groups were broken down, and therapists such as Carl Rogers made their interpersonal skills and theoretical approaches available to persons not necessarily identified as patients. Growth and human potential centers such as Esalen in California opened their doors to human beings—not just "students" or "patients"—who wanted to increase their awareness of themselves and improve their ability to relate to other human beings. Emphasis on the human experience—the happy and unhappy, the adaptive and maladaptive parts in all of us—has definitely led to a theoretical confusion of what is treatment, what is learning, and what is human encounter. Today there are groups available for almost everything. People can lose weight, quit smoking, learn to be more effective parents, obtain a divorce, learn natural childbirth, be cured of their neuroses, improve their management skills, share common uncomfortable experiences, learn to emote, etc., etc., etc. in groups.

It is into this seemingly theoretical confusion about groups that I wish to insert nursing practice. In answering the questions, Why use groups?, What types of groups are available?, and How do groups help people?, a foundation will be laid for the assessment of small group objectives. Methods of describing and categorizing various types of groups will be discussed and emphasis will be given to the therapeutic use of groups in the delivery of nursing care to clients.

REFERENCES

1. Lewin, K.: Forces behind food habits and methods of change, Bull. Natl. Res. Counc. **108**:35-65, 1943.
2. White, R., and Lippitt, R.: Leader behavior and member reaction in three "social climates." In Cartwright, D., and Zander, A. (eds.): Group dynamics, New York, 1968, Harper & Row, Publishers.

1 □ Why use groups?
CLIENT NEEDS

Nurses are concerned with affecting the health behavior of clients. In its simplest form this involves either the maintenance of existing behaviors, the alteration of existing behaviors, and/or the learning of new behaviors on the part of the client. Groups can be utilized to meet a variety of client needs related to their biopsychosocial health behaviors.

SUPPORT

Many people already practice good physical and emotional health behaviors. With these persons, the nurse's role is that of assisting them to monitor and maintain their health status. Especially during periods of change or crisis, the support of other people can help clients to adjust to the change, handle the crisis, or maintain their adaptive or healthy behaviors. That is why nurses have begun organizing group meetings for parents with a child in the hospital or groups for people adjusting to divorce or being a single parent. It is not that these people do not know or cannot determine what to do; the benefit of the group lies more in the mutual support and sharing of common experiences by people who are in similar situations.

The reports of people who have participated in such groups indicate that these common support groups have preventive potential. That is, they prevent the development of maladaptive patterns of coping and help to maintain the healthy behaviors of the group members. One such person, a recently divorced woman with two preschool children reported that the support she received from her crisis group and the opportunity to discuss her plans with other women in a similar situation helped her to decide that she was not a bad mother for arranging to enroll her children in a day-care program so that she could complete her college degree. The group confirmed her thinking that she was a person with her own needs and aspirations and that obtaining her degree and the subsequent career opportunities would both materially and emotionally enhance her ability to care for herself and her children. This woman received help from the group in dealing with her feelings about an adaptive plan that she herself had devised. Her comment after six sessions in the divorce group was, "I don't think I would have done it without the group support. They helped me believe in myself at a time when I was seriously questioning my own abilities."

TASK ACCOMPLISHMENT

Certain tasks cannot be accomplished alone. Certainly the delivery of modern health care is a constant example of the professional interdependence and cooperation required in our society. The more complex the task, the more likely that it will require a group or multiple groups of people to produce the final product. Individuals with unique skills and attributes must come together, agree on the goal and how it will be reached, and then work together to accomplish it. During this process they must learn to respect and value each other's differences as well as their similarities.

Nurses can make use of this ability of groups to accomplish complex tasks. Very often a group of clients can be brought together in a manner that maximizes their problem-solving capabilities and advances the health care goals of the client. On one inpatient psychiatric ward the nurse was able to gather a group of patients interested in redecorating the day room. Utilizing their collective skills, the group broke the redecorating project down into its component parts and divided tasks among subgroups. With minimal guidance from the nurse, the subgroups conducted a car wash to raise the necessary funds, planned the colors and fabrics to be used in decorating, purchased the materials, paint, etc. for the project, and spent their free time on the ward sewing, painting, and rebuilding furniture. Within 2 months the redecorating project was completed with minimal expense to the hospital and a maximum sense of accomplishment on the part of the patients in the group.

Such task-oriented groups can also be used to therapeutic advantage in teaching patients to work together when this is a useful treatment outcome. In the situation described above, several more disturbed patients were able to work along with the patient subgroups and learned how to plan and carry out such a project. This type of goal-directed, collaborative behavior can be an essential learning technique in the rehabilitation of some patients.

In a community health agency another nurse recognized the need for greater community acceptance and understanding of the needs of the older adult. Instead of mounting such a campaign herself, she enlisted several senior citizen groups in developing and implementing the project. Not only were the ideas and information that resulted more relevant to the actual experience of the older adults, but there was a definite benefit to the older clients that resulted from participating in their own public awareness campaign. The campaign gave these clients an outlet for their interests and provided many enjoyable hours of useful activity. Several ongoing projects resulted from the involvement of the older adults in the public awareness campaign. One of these projects was an adopted grandparents service whereby families in the community who wanted their children to have contact with an older adult "adopted" a "grandparent" who contracted for inclusion in certain family activities. In this manner the needs of both the older adults and the younger people in the community were satisfied.

SOCIALIZATION

Very few people can or want to live in isolation from other people. For most people in our society social contact with other people is a source of reinforcement and enjoyment. When something happens to disrupt this social source of satisfaction people become depressed or eventually exhibit some form of maladaptive behavior. Depression very often occurs when a person loses someone or something that has been a source of reinforcement and self-affirmation. Loss of a close relative or friend, divorce, graduation, moving to a new location, or retirement are a few of the personal events that can produce a sense of loss and depression. The person who is experiencing the loss can be helped to seek out new or alternative sources of interpersonal satisfaction if the nurse is aware of this need. Since groups are comprised of other people, they are often a source of interpersonal reinforcement.

Parents Without Partners is an example of a social group that assists divorced or widowed persons to obtain support from others sharing a common experience as well as to make new social contacts and develop new sources of interpersonal reinforcement. Other groups such as the YMCA and YWCA, Big Brother Program, community athletic teams, skill and craft clubs, and retirement community groups are all examples of potentially therapeutic groups. Nurses who are aware of the needs of their clients as well as the available community resources can make good use of these groups to meet the socialization needs of their clients. People who have been removed from society or who have experienced a different type of social contact for a time require resocialization opportunities. Viet Nam veterans, discharged mental patients, and ex-prisoners all represent persons for whom a resocialization experience should be planned. One example of such groups is the aftercare groups available in some community mental health centers. In these groups discharged patients who have been hospitalized for emotional problems can share experiences and learn new ways of coping with the re-entry process into society. Discussion topics often include how to become reacquainted with old friends, interviewing for a job, and conversing socially at group gatherings or parties. Following a brief aftercare experience these people are much better prepared to resume their role as members of naturally occurring social groups.

LEARNING–BEHAVIOR CHANGE

Since nurses are concerned with affecting the health behavior of clients, they are necessarily involved with the alteration of existing unhealthy behaviors and the learning of new, healthier behaviors. Patients with hypertension, a new pacemaker, or diabetes are just a few of the types of patients who need to learn about their condition. Each of them is expected to learn a new diet, adjust their work and activities to their physical condition, and learn about their medications, possible side effects, and when to seek medical or nursing assistance. Not only do they need information that can be transmitted more efficiently in a group than on a one-to-one basis, but they also need to alter certain of their pre-illness behaviors to implement their treatment plan. The study by Lewin[1] provides one of the earliest demonstrations of the effectiveness of utilizing groups to produce behavior change. Women who made a commitment as a group to increase their family's consumption of organ meats followed through and changed their shopping and cooking behaviors at a higher rate than women who were provided with information and made no such group commitment.

The implications of this study for the teaching of patients who need to alter their diets because of diabetes, hypertension, renal disease, and the like are obvious. If the nurse can transmit information to patients in a group and then obtain a group commitment to behavior change, the probabilities are greater that the patients will actually follow through. There is a need for nursing research to explore this group phenomenon with various client groups in different settings. It is possible that the clients will need an ongoing group contact to maintain their newly learned behaviors. Again, there is a need for research to determine the length and extent of group follow-up required for permanent change.

Numerous groups already exist that deal with health care learning and behavior change. Weight Watchers International is a private corporation with branches in many local communities that makes use of group commitment and group reinforcement to assist people in losing weight and maintaining this weight loss. Lamaze techniques of natural childbirth are usually taught in group classes. Parent Effectiveness Training and Parents Anonymous are two more examples of approaches that make use of group techniques to facilitate learning and behavioral change on the part of parents. Since these groups are basically set up as teaching-learning experiences, it may be useful with certain clients to utilize them as an adjunct to counselling or treatment experiences. This point will be discussed further in Chapter 2.

HUMAN RELATIONS TRAINING

Since its inception in the mid-1940s, human relations training has experienced what can only be termed an "explosion" in the numbers and types of training available throughout the United States. First developed in Bethel, Maine, by Leland Bradford, Ronald Lippitt, and Kenneth Benne, the original human relations laboratories were designed as 3-week workshop experiences for professional persons who wanted to learn more effective techniques for dealing with the human relations problems they encountered in their jobs.

The most popular and apparently interpersonally rewarding component of these human relations laboratories was the "basic skills training groups" (shortened in 1949 to "T-group") that met with a leader, called the trainer, and an observer. These sessions were divided into two parts; the first part was a discussion of back-home problems, and the second part was a feedback period during which the observer shared his process observations of the ways in which the participants had expressed themselves and affected the other group members. This unique opportunity to directly give and receive feedback provided such an emotionally charged experience for the participants that the laboratory leaders experienced considerable pressure to expand the T-group into all aspects of the workshop. By 1950, the National Training Laboratory (NTL) was established within the National Education Association as a permanent, year-round organization. Over the next 20 years its activities spread beyond Bethel, Maine to numerous regional branches and by the late 1960s NTL was reaching over 2,500 workshop participants a year.

What is important to note is not just the growth of NTL, but the concomitant growth of human relations training prompted by and reflected in the proliferation of the T-group. To even the most casual observer, it is clear that in our production-oriented, role-specific society there are few available experiences in which people feel free to be themselves, to admit to their insecure feelings as well as their professional competencies. By and large, people have become more distant and less human with each other. If this were not true, the T-group and subsequent human relations, or encounter group, movement would not have caught on to the degree that it has. One must assume that people in our society within the past 30 years have been experiencing an increasing need for a forum for sharing their humanness with each other.

As mentioned earlier, human relations training was originally designed to be a learning or educational experience for teachers, administrators, counselors, and others whose jobs required some degree of facility for dealing with people. By the mid 1960s the encounter group movement was advertising itself as providing group therapy for "normal" people, and the distinction between a complete educational experience and therapy was considerably blurred. However, some distinct attributes of the human relations group do remain that can be discussed in a general manner.

First and foremost, the focus on human relations training remains educational. Human relations groups are usually comprised of persons who have come together for a specified number of hours or sessions with the expressed purpose of learning something both cognitively and experientially about human relations. The fact that some people who would be better served by psychotherapy attempt to deal with their problems in a human relations group need not obscure the original educational intent of the group. The basic objective of the human relations group is interpersonal competence, and the group is structured in such a manner as to help its participants deal openly with their "here and now" relationships in the group, receive corrective feedback on the effect they have on themselves and others, and to transfer these learnings into the "real world" settings to which they will return.

Leaders of human relations groups often have a variety of professional and educational backgrounds. Many professional programs for psychotherapists have in fact provided for human relations groups as a part of their training program. Basically, however, the human relations trainer, or group leader, is a person specially trained in group process and the utilization of specific techniques for assisting people to become aware of themselves and the impact they have on other people. Programs such as the NTL train T-group trainers, and it is important to inquire about the academic and training background of the leader before becoming involved in one of the numerous human relations groups available. In some settings, especially college towns or university settings, there is a confusing multiplicity of encounter-type groups available. It is wise, not naive, to ask questions about the leader and the techniques to be utilized before referring clients or making a personal commitment to participate. Assertiveness training, T-groups, body workshops, Tai Chi, emotive therapy, and sexuality experiences can vary markedly depending on the training and skills of the leader.

One of the important assets of a well-run human relations group is the powerful experience that is available with a safe leader and a group contract to be open and direct with the people involved. So few people regularly experience such an open commitment to sharing themselves in their social and work contacts that the human relations group experience is often unique and energizing. Learning about human relations can occur in the group and can be generalized to home, social, and work relationships, especially if this generalization is planned. This type of learning needs to occur in groups where people can demonstrate their current manner of relating, receive honest feedback, and practice and experience new methods of relating to other people.

PSYCHOTHERAPY—INSIGHT AND BEHAVIOR CHANGE

Psychotherapy groups are yet another category in the vast array of groups available to clients. In comparison with the preceding description of human relations training groups, therapy groups also have a focus and technique of their own. In the simplest terms, therapy groups are concerned with the "treatment" of "patients" and are conducted by a "therapist" with the objectives of "insight" and/or "behavioral change." As the reader can readily discern, this explanation does not immediately clarify the confusion.

The origins of group psychotherapy lie within the group application of the theories of the various schools of psychotherapy—Freudian, Sullivanian, Rogerian, Bernien. As therapists who had been trained in one of the numerous theories of psychotherapy began to apply their treatment frameworks in groups, they also began to work together conceptually to develop specific techniques of group therapy. The convergence of group psychotherapy with the encounter group movement of the 1960s has already been mentioned along with the resultant blurring of what constitutes treatment of psychopathology and what constitutes human relations training for "normal" people. Indeed, today many "normal" people who are experiencing no extreme difficulty in functioning or meeting their interpersonal or professional responsibilities are involved as clients in psychotherapy groups. Often these "normal" people who come for psychotherapy are interested in understanding themselves better or in quelling a vague uneasiness or dissatisfaction with themselves and their relationships.

As the definition of normal versus mentally ill becomes more and more socially defined, it becomes increasingly difficult to define therapy groups by their sick versus healthy membership. One must look within the process and techniques of the group to begin to make distinctions. Although there are always problems with overgeneralizing, therapy groups are, by and large, for people who are dissatisfied and want to change something about themselves. They may be self-referred or sent by a family member or social agency, but usually there is some motivating force that defines the need for change. This does not preclude the occasional group member who, once confronted with the possibility of change, decides that he is either not ready or not willing to change. The process of change, whether implicit or explicit, in most treatment groups often requires that the client develop some degree of insight regarding himself and his problems. This intrapersonal and interpersonal insight at times resembles and is similar to the interpersonal learning that occurs in human relations training groups and therefore adds to the confusion between the two. Some therapy groups rely on the clients achieving insight into themselves and their relationships, while others expect that the insight, once achieved, will result in or lead to some sort of behavioral change. It is safe to say that since most people are participating in group therapy to produce some sort of feeling or behavioral change, the most common group therapy expectation is that the client will achieve more than just insight.

Therapy groups are led by therapists who usually have a graduate degree in nursing, medicine, social work, or psychology as well as supervised experience and training in group psychotherapy. Depending on the theoretical orientation of the therapist, the group may focus on the intrapersonal and/or interpersonal problems of the client. The group is viewed as a social microcosm in which the clients demonstrate their problematic feelings and behaviors and in which they can experience the corrective emotional experience of being responded to differently. Within this context, the therapist assumes a parental role in helping patients learn new ways of coping.

Labeling the above process "psychotherapy" may cause some concern on the part of those who consider support, task accomplishment, socialization, learning–behavior change, and human relations training to be therapeutic. Indeed, all of these approaches can have therapeutic value. Psychotherapy, however, is different in that it focuses on the goal-directed alteration of how the client relates himself and others in an overall way. Psychotherapy may include altering specific behaviors or learning new ways of relating to other people, but it also includes specific assistance with how one feels about oneself. In this way it is not better than other types of group intervention, merely different. Psychotherapy is facilitated within a group setting because of the presence of people in addition to the client and the therapist. The specific mechanisms of change in group therapy are discussed in Chapter 3. For the moment, it is sufficient to indicate that there is research to support the fact that group therapy works equally as well as other forms of psychotherapy. The major influencing factor appears to be the effectiveness of the therapist, regardless of theoretical orientation of the group.

In summary, a variety of client needs can be met in groups. The general categories of clinet need discussed are support, task accomplishment, socialization, learning–behavior change, human relations training, and psychotherapy. The majority of client needs confronted by the nurse can be readily identified as fitting into one of these categories. We will return to these categories later as we attempt to more systematically describe the structure, process, and outcomes of utilizing groups for health care intervention.

REFERENCE

1. Lewin, K.: Forces behind food habits and methods of change, Bull. Natl. Res. Coun. **108:**35-65, 1943.

2 □ Why use groups?
ASSESSMENT ISSUES

THERAPIST OBJECTIVES

In addition to the various client needs enumerated in Chapter 1, certain objectives of the nurse-leader must be considered in answering the question, "Why use groups?" The specific outcomes nurses expect for their clients are discussed in Chapter 3 and are correlated with the various types of groups. Several general advantages to the use of groups for meeting the nurse's objectives with clients are discussed here.

Groups are often considered to be a more economical mode of intervention. A greater number of clients can be reached at one time, resulting in a more efficient use of the nurse's time and energy. After all, if you have to teach a diabetic diet to one client, why not teach it to ten at the same time? In an aftercare clinic that treats a large number of newly discharged state hospital patients, a group of ten or twelve clients can receive an hour of the nurse's attention rather than the usual 5 minutes per visit.

The validity of this economy concept does need to be questioned. Depending on the size of the group, the type of client, and the nature of the group activity, a group may require co-leaders to maximize the therapeutic benefit. This automatically cuts the economy factor in half. Further, group interventions tend to be more energy-consuming of the leader since there are more clients and interactional issues that require the leader's attention. Most group leaders believe that two groups, or three at the most, per day is all that they can handle. If time is allotted for practice or feedback from each group member, the length of the group session must be adjusted accordingly. For instance, a class for diabetic clients in which all clients demonstrate their proficiency in self-administration of an insulin injection requires more time than a session in which the same group receives a lecture on proper skin care.

The health care objectives that can be accomplished in groups are much more important than the economical use of the nurse's time and energy or the fact that more clients can be reached in a shorter period. The primary advantage of a group lies in the composition of the group itself—the fact that a variety of people with similar problems or objectives are working on them together. This experience of the commonality of problems within a group often has therapeutic value in and of itself. It helps the group members to break through their barrier of aloneness and isolation and experience a mutual concern with other human beings. The sharing of common human concerns may occur in a group of amputees who are discussing their difficulties with obtaining consistent employment, in a group of parents whose children are hospitalized for major surgery, or in a group of recent retirees. Regardless of the grouping of clients or the problem being solved, the sharing of basic human problems is one of the basic benefits.

When clients share their concerns related to their health care situation, the response of the other group members is striking. Because the group is composed of a variety of individuals, group members can receive a wide variety of feedback. This feedback may range from very specific suggestions such as how to arrange one's kitchen so that meal preparation is facilitated to a statement of interpersonal support that others have felt or are feeling. Feedback of this nature often has more potency because it is being offered by others who share similar problems or experiences. Some nurses have been surprised to discover that the same suggestion made by them 2 weeks earlier is suddenly accepted when offered by another group member.

Small groups are often referred to as social microcosms, because eventually group members will demonstrate their problems within the group. The client who is having difficulty in presenting himself in a positive light during job interviews will also demonstrate his low self-esteem in the group. The group members can then share their reactions to the client's helpless-hopeless demeanor and offer constructive suggestions about how to change. The range of possible feedback is greater in a group than if this same client were talking individually with the nurse. While it is likely to take more than one session for this client to change both his self-concept and his behavior, the support, cohesiveness, and consistent pressure of the group often facilitates the change process. Many perspectives on both the problem and its solution are available.

While a group functions as a social microcosm with respect to the assessment of client problems, with the guidance of a skilled leader it is unique in its ability to respond supportively and constructively to promote change. Very few potential employers will take the time or concern necessary to deal with an applicant's discouraging presentation of himself. He simply will not get the job. The group, on the other hand, can be guided to give the client a range of feedback on the consequences of his behavior as well as constructive assistance with the process of change. The group also provides a valuable testing ground for trying out new behaviors and offers a large quantity of direct reinforcement for behavioral change. Within the group, the client can demonstrate his improved sense of himself in his interactions with the other group members. He can also role-play future job interview situations as a way of perfecting his new-found skills.

The role of the nurse-leader in the group is that of facilitator and not that of single curative agent. As a health care provider, the nurse is available as an "expert" for the group, but the nurse's primary function is that of assisting the group members to utilize each other. In fact, group intervention is often the treatment of choice for clients who tend to form very dependent relationships with one exclusive person. The group can be utilized to decrease dependence on the leader and increase the client's reliance on a variety of interpersonal and social resources.

Persons who share a common health problem, such as undergoing a mastectomy or colostomy, will often maintain contact following termination of a group experience. In some communities these persons have formed clubs or groups of their own to provide health education for the public and support and information to other persons undergoing similar procedures. There appears to be some therapeutic value not only in receiving the support of the group, but also in being able to share one's own experiences and support with others. Some organizations, such as Alcoholics Anonymous, have made excellent use of a member's ability to help others with similar problems as a therapeutic process.

The nurse-leader should consider all of the above advantages when deciding on group intervention for discussing a general or specific health care issue. The group can be a potent vehicle for therapeutic change if organized in such a way as to maximize this potential for sharing among its members.

SYSTEM EXPECTATIONS

It is important to consider the expectations of the health care delivery system during the developmental stages of a group form of intervention.

The objectives and expectations of the facility or agency can·greatly affect the advantages of any health care group formed under its auspices by its professional staff. For example, I have worked on an inpatient psychiatric unit in which individual psychotherapy was considered to be the most valuable form of treatment. Group psychotherapy, ward activities groups, recreational groups, and ward community meetings all took a backseat to the 2 to 3 hours of individual psychotherapy per week received by each patient. No attempt was made to formulate a treatment plan regarding specific patient outcomes and the relative effectiveness of various treatment modalities in accomplishing these objectives. Several comparison studies were even proposed to measure the effects of individual, group, and milieu (living situation) therapy, but to no avail. The overall value system placed priority on individual psychotherapy.

Therapy groups were established within this setting but were usually regarded as a secondary form of treatment. Activities or learning groups organized by the nursing staff were seen as helpful, but insufficient methods of helping patients. This value system did not prevent the formation of therapy and activities groups, but the nurses who organized them did so with the full understanding that they could anticipate only minimal support and assistance from "the system."

The system can often offer some interesting answers to the question of why to use groups. Health care agencies and facilities have economic and public relations objectives that are not always shared by clinicians. They operate under a formal charter or constitution that ascribes to them certain general health care functions, and they must accomplish these functions within a certain budget and maintain a critical mass of public confidence and support. The public or community attributes to the agency or facility certain capabilities for meeting their health care needs and will attempt to hold the organization publicly accountable. The professional staff within the facility or agency assumes that their role is to meet the health care needs of a specific or general client population. Since they are conscientious, professional people, they also assume that they know best how to meet the needs of their clients. The outcomes of their health care interventions are not always monitored to determine what they are actually accomplishing.

So far, the system seems pretty manageable. What can and does happen, however, is that what is expected by the system, the public, and the professional and the actual outcomes are not in harmony. These discrepancies can affect the use of groups as vehicles for health care. For example, the hospital administrator may not be able to demonstrate or understand the cost/benefit ratio of self-care groups led by the gynecology nurse practitioner. What the administrator sees is that the 4 hours per week that the nurse is spending with these groups could be used to increase the number of pelvic examinations done in the clinic. On the other hand, the nurse working in a counselling position with renal dialysis clients may receive pressure to work with them in a group to utilize the time more efficiently.

In a mental health clinic situation, clients may expect to be assigned their own nurse whom they can see individually at least once a week. Despite the nurse's explanation of the advantages of a group, it may be difficult to convince these clients that they are not receiving second-rate treatment. On the inpatient psychiatric unit mentioned previously, this message was further reinforced by the prevailing values of the more influential professional staff and irregular attendance at group sessions was a persistent problem.

These problematic situations are mentioned only as a caution regarding the effect the larger health care system can have on the objectives of health care groups. A system that is totally supportive of group interventions can greatly facilitate their therapeutic potential. A system that is not supportive can minimize or even block the effectiveness of the group.

DISADVANTAGES OF GROUPS

The disadvantages of using groups to deliver health care to clients should at least be mentioned. The major disadvantages of groups stem from the misuse or misdirection of the previously discussed advantages. Each of these advantages can be turned into a disadvantage if the therapist lacks the knowledge and skill required to work with groups.

It has been proposed that groups can be utilized by the nurse to reach a greater number of clients at one time, resulting in a more efficient use of the nurse's time and energy. It is also possible to establish a group with too large a membership to accomplish the primary goal of the group. For example, if the objective of the group is one that requires that a great deal of individual attention be paid to group members, the group needs to be small enough to permit this attention. Such is the case in a group where skills are being taught. If colostomy irrigation is being learned, the nurse must be able to work with each client individually as well as in the group. Usually when the number of clients exceeds six, the nurse should either start a second group or obtain assistance. It is a mistake to attempt to deal with too many clients at one time; this often results in a decrease in the amount of learning that is possible.

The nurse-leader or therapist needs to feel comfortable in working with groups of clients. Bringing a number of people with common problems together as a group is not enough. The leader must provide the structure and guide the process that is to occur within the group. In this context, the group is only as good as its leader. Much more attention is given to the group leader in Section III.

There are also some physical arrangement problems that can become disadvantages of working with clients in groups. In some settings it can be extremely difficult to find a time when all the clients are free from other treatment activities to participate in a group. In a hospital, for instance, many of the daytime hours are filled with clinic, physical therapy, or radiation therapy appointments. Evenings are usually reserved for visitors and the group leader is left to somehow discover a common free hour or two that will not conflict with the essentials of hospital routine.

Finding a room that is adequate in size and privacy can also be a problem, since most facilities have not been designed with group therapy or client classroom space in mind. One group of hospitalized, physically ill adolescents was able to reserve the ward game room for an hour block of time twice a week. Besides the lack of privacy, this arrangement also required a great deal of time of the nurse therapist. The nurse therapist arrived on the ward an hour before the group began to remind the youngsters, to move chairs and tables from the middle of the game room, and then to transport all of the nonambulatory group members to the game room. Following the group this same process was repeated in reverse as the youngsters were returned to their rooms, the game room rearranged, and any postgroup upsets followed up with the youngster and the nursing staff. Thus, a 1-hour group session actually required 3 to 4 hours of the leader's time. The clinical specialist conducting this group certainly needed to be committed to the therapeutic value of working with adolescents in groups.

There are also certain group process problems that, if not handled well, can become disadvantages of working with clients in groups. The point has already been made that there is great advantage in bringing together a variety of people with common problems or objectives to work together on their solution. It is also possible that, once together, this group of clients will share a common resistance to change. For example, in an aftercare group several clients may join together to lead a group discussion of how awful it is being a former state hospital patient. The group leader needs to know how to turn this discussion around so that the clients not only vent their anger at this situation but also have the opportunity to discuss what they can do to alter their current situation. There is little advantage to a gripe session if it does not lead to some more positive behavioral outcome.

Once a group resistance to change has built up, it is difficult for the group members not to go along with the group norms. In their discomfort, the group members can actually wind up supporting weaknesses rather than strengths. To illustrate, in a group of recently divorced women with young children, one of the more assertive members persisted over several sessions in developing her case to prove that "all men are bastards." She captured the natural anger of the other group members who were still hurting from their recent losses, and for three consecutive sessions the group members left feeling worse than when they had arrived. In the fourth session, the group leader was able to interest the group in a discussion of why they had been feeling worse instead of better following the group meetings and several members were able to express their disappointment. Then one of the women began to cry and shared with the other members the frustration she was experiencing over not getting her needs met in the group. The leader then pointed out the similarities between what had occurred in the group and what had occurred in their marriages, and the group began to determine ways in which they could get their needs met both inside and outside the group.

Another component of the group process that may seem to be a disadvantage is the apparent lack of individual attention of the therapist to each group member. This lack of individual attention can become a problem if the leader and/or the group members are not convinced that it is the group and not just the leader that can help people change. In this situation the leader must remain aware of the desire of the members for special attention, point out this process, and redirect the discussion back to the group. The leader who chooses to be the only expert in the group is minimizing the advantages of enlisting group members to help each other.

ASSESSMENT QUESTIONS

The question, Why use groups?, has been discussed from a variety of perspectives in the preceding sections. In discussing the variables of client needs, therapist objectives, system expectations, and disadvantages of groups, a beginning foundation has been laid for the assessment of small group objectives. This is, in fact, the most basic level in assessing whether or not to use a small group approach in dealing with the health care needs of clients.

The nurse must begin by asking a series of questions.

1. *What are the client needs I am attempting to meet?*

Utilizing the categories proposed earlier, the nurse needs to make some determination of the health care need(s) the client is attempting to meet.

The best and most effective way to make this determination is to involve the client. Very often clients know or can be helped to become aware of their own needs relative to their biopsychosocial health status. In a dialogue with the nurse, clients can make use of the nurse's professional expertise to clarify their own health care objectives.

It is important for the nurse and client to arrive at a mutual understanding of whether the client need is for support, task accomplishment, socialization, learning-behavior change, human relations training, or psychotherapy. If there are several client needs to be met, some determination can be made as to whether these objectives can be accomplished separately or simultaneously in a single group.

2. *Can these needs be met in a group?*

The initial consideration in answering this question is whether or not the client and the nurse think the identified client needs can be met in a group. Actually, there are very few needs that cannot be met in a group if the client and nurse are inclined to utilize group interventions. If the client is uncomfortable in dealing with a specific problem in a group setting and cannot be persuaded otherwise, a group is not appropriate. The situation may also exist in which there is no appropriate group readily available to meet the client's needs.

Generally speaking, however, the only client needs that are difficult to meet in a group setting are needs for a one-to-one relationship. At times, clients (adults and children) who have not learned to trust or relate intimately with another person are very much in need of an individual relationship. While this need can be met in some groups, it is usually desirable to work with these persons individually. For example, an autistic child must first learn to trust and relate to one caring adult before he is able to move on to multiple relationships with adults or other children. For certain retarded adults, the stimulation of a group is too great initially and they must first begin to relate to one person at a time.

3. *What are my own (or the other therapist's) objectives for the proposed group?*

The therapist's objectives for the proposed group intervention need to be clearly stated and assessed. If they are considering the formation of a new group to meet the needs of a certain client population, the nurses need to be clear about their own expectations of the outcomes. What need(s) are they attempting to meet, and what are their own objectives for establishing the group? What are the therapeutic advantages versus disadvantages of working with these clients in a group? Do the nurses possess the skills and have access to the necessary supervision for working with the group? More will be discussed in Section II regarding the specific considerations in establishing a group. For the purposes of discussing the assessment of small group objectives, the above considerations are sufficient.

If the nurse is considering a client referral to an already established group, the above questions should be asked of the leader or therapist. It is important to know what client needs the group leader is attempting to meet and what objectives are held for the group. Some attempt should be made to determine the degree to which the leader will engage the group membership in meeting the overall group objectives.

4. *What are the expectations of the system relative to the proposed group?*

Before initiating a new group or referring clients to an existing group, it is important that nurses assess the expectations of the system or organization in which they are working. What is the value system of the health care agency or facility regarding group treatment or learning experiences? Does sufficient support exist for the proposed group to help the nurse in establishing and working with the group. Unfortunately there are far too many examples of health care teaching groups or client counselling groups that are run by nurses who come in on their free time because the agency does not value the group enough to include it in the nurse's normal work expectations. Eventually, the excitement of leading such a group without the active support of the agency wears thin. There are enough problems to solve in the process of establishing and conducting such a group that the full support of the facility or agency is essential to the viability of the group.

5. *Is there any discrepancy or conflict between the answers to questions 1 through 4?*

If the answer to this question is "no," the course of action is clear. Ideally, the client needs, the usefulness of a group in meeting those needs, the objectives of the therapist, and the expectations of the system all coalesce to provide for a uniform set of small group objectives.

If a discrepancy does exist among the client needs, the usefulness of a group in meeting those needs, the objectives of the therapist, and the expectations of the system, the nurse and client need to reconsider. If a group would not be useful in meeting the identified client needs, some other form of intervention should be considered. If no group currently exists, some determination should be made of the potential client population for a group to meet the identified client needs. If the objectives of the therapist do not match the client needs, an alternative group should be found. If the client has several needs, a decision must be made regarding the one or several group experiences in which they can be met. If the health care system or organization holds different expectations for client treatment than those shared by the client and nurse, some determination should be made regarding the relative advantages, disadvantages and risks of proceeding versus formulating an alternative plan.

The decision of whether or not to utilize a group approach in meeting the health care needs of clients will still come down to the best judgment of the nurse, client, or others involved in the situation. By clearly answering the above questions, the nurse should be able to gain some assessment information that will assist in making an informed decision.

3 □ Types of available groups

Literally hundreds of different types of groups are currently or potentially available to clients. It is possible, and at times advantageous, to look at each separate group as a distinct entity in attempting to determine whether or not it will meet the specific needs of a specific client. There is also something to be gained in attempting to categorize available and potential groups into certain categories. For one thing, categories help to focus the student's thinking about the similar and dissimilar aspects of various groups. Categorizing groups also helps the clinician and client to bring some order to the apparent public and professional chaos that exists regarding which modality or which group will actually meet the clients' needs.

When professionals and lay persons become confused about the wide variety of available health care groups, it is usually because they are using a set of mixed variables to describe the group. Why is it that interpersonal learning is the objective of sensitivity–encounter groups, yet interpersonal learning also occurs in most psychotherapy groups? What is the difference between a supportive psychotherapy group and an emotional support group that has therapeutic elements?

This section attempts to develop a clear model for categorizing groups. This model is presented as a beginning reference point for understanding the multitude of available health care groups. As with most models, it assumes that the world is neat and orderly. This is obviously not the case in most instances. Following the presentation of the model, attention will be given to the types of mixed variable groups that develop in many health care settings. A variety of methods exist for describing and categorizing health care groups. Each of these methods of categorization is based on a different set of variables that occur in the group. The four most common group descriptors are (1) objectives, (2) structure, (3) process, and (4) outcomes. These group descriptors will be discussed separately.

GROUP OBJECTIVES

Groups can be categorized according to their major objective. An *emotional support* group will have as its primary objective the support and maintenance of existing strengths. No attempt will be made to alter the members' feelings or behaviors, and the group will focus on reassurance and reinforcement of its members personal and environmental resources.

A group that has a primary *task* orientation will focus its attentions on the completion of the task. The group will select its members for their ability to contribute to accomplishing the primary task, and its activities will be clearly goal directed. Eventually, task groups also need to give attention to the interpersonal needs of their members and develop ways in which the work process can go smoothly. The primary reason, however, for attending to the interpersonal group process is so that the task objective can be accomplished.

Socialization groups will be concerned with the social and interactional compatibility of their membership. When such a social club is formed, the activities chosen by the members will be those that provide them with social enjoyment. A *learning* group, on the other hand, often forms around a very specific interest or need area. People who want to lose weight, learn a skill, or become more effective parents will find others with a similar interest and develop a mechanism for learning or changing their behavior. This usually involves engaging a teacher or leader who can help them to accomplish their stated objective.

Sensitivity–encounter groups can be viewed as an even more specific type of learning group where the objective is to learn about interpersonal and human relations. Because of this objective, members are selected who will deal in the here and now with what is going on among themselves and the other group members.

Psychotherapy groups have as their objective the examination and alteration of intrapersonal as well as interpersonal relationships of their members. The intrapersonal objective requires examining how the person feels, thinks, and relates to himself. The interpersonal objective deals with the person's relationships with other people in the group as well as in the rest of his personal and professional life.

Once having presented this listing of fairly specific group objectives, it is important to recognize that many health care groups are attempting to accomplish more than one type of objective. The same activity can be designed to accomplish one or several objectives. For example, a group that is set up to teach natural childbirth may consider emotional support to be an equally important objective. An activity group may plan a trip to an amusement park as a means of teaching the members to plan a group activity or as a means of encouraging socialization, or both. A socialization group may decide that there is a mutually agreed upon task they would like to accomplish such as raising funds to send underprivileged children to camp or participating in a specific learning experience together, such as learning to deal with their adolescent children's drug problems. It is important to realize when a group is attempting to accomplish more than one type of objective because this has implications for the type of group process in which they will engage. More about this will be presented in the discussion of group process.

GROUP STRUCTURE

The second group descriptor that can be used to explain different types of groups is the structure of the group itself. Very often it is useful to explain the objectives of the group and then to describe the group structure in terms of the following parameters. Each of these parameters says something about the group above and beyond its objectives.

The *type of clients* who are members of the group is one of the most important structural considerations. The importance of group membership is highlighted by some clinicians who believe that the group will move only as fast as its slowest member. While this idea has not been substantiated by research, one cannot ignore the issue of abilities of group members to contribute to the group objectives. Most groups are structured so that the type of client taken into the group is consistent with the group objectives. A group whose objective is learning and behavior change will require the selection of clients who share this objective. Thus, some initial attempt will be made to select clients who want to learn and change.

Another important structural consideration for health care groups is the *level of prevention* that the group is trying to achieve. The level of prevention is closely related to the type of client to be considered for group membership. One would not consider placing clients who have come to learn about breast cancer detection procedures (primary prevention) with clients who are dealing with the grief and altered body image following a mastectomy (secondary prevention) or with clients who are sharing their experience of having terminal cancer (tertiary prevention). The needs of the clients and the objectives of the group at these different levels of prevention are fairly incompatible.

The *degree of structure* that is provided within the group can be viewed as occurring along a continuum from very structured to very loose and unstructured. Groups can be placed all along this continuum depending on the degree to which the internal functioning of the group follows a predictable, predetermined agenda. Perhaps the clearest example of a very structured group is a task group or organization that strictly adheres to an agenda and a set of operating rules of order. On the other end of the structure continuum is a very open, leaderless process group where the members come together to process and experience each other and the only predetermined structure is the time and place of their meeting.

Since some clients want and/or need to be able to predict what will happen in the group, it is important that the nurse and client discuss the parameters of structure before the client enters the group. Children's activity groups can require a fair amount of initial structure depending on the developmental age of the members. Within this structure, opportunities need to be provided for the physical and emotional expression appropriate to the children's developmental needs. Learning–behavior change groups usually have a predetermined structure to most of their activities so that the information to be learned can be presented and practiced. Psychotherapy groups will vary in the amount of structure depending on the type of clients and the theoretical orientation of the therapist. For example, actively psychotic clients require more control and structure from the therapist than does a group of outpatients who are in therapy to learn to deal with their anxieties and depressions related to their daily personal and professional lives.

The *theoretical orientation* of the group and its leader or therapist can also be used to explain what will occur in the group. A weight loss group whose leader makes use of the principles of operant learning theory will utilize techniques such as reinforcement of weight loss and careful monitoring of eating behavior to achieve the stated objective. On the other hand, a more interpersonally oriented leader may choose to focus on what use the clients are making of their obesity in relating to other people. Both groups may accomplish the objective of weight loss through the use of different methodologies related to their theoretical orientation.

The theoretical orientation of the leader also affects the degree of structure that is utilized during the course of the group sessions. Operant conditioning or learning theory uses a very specific and structured approach to the monitoring and alteration of behaviorally defined desirable and undesirable outcomes. On the other hand, Freudian or psychoanalytically oriented therapists tend to rely on the evolution of group process and the interventions of the therapist are focused on the interpretation of group and individual behaviors as they evolve. In this latter example, too much imposed group structure would interfere with the development of process issues within the group.

Groups can also be described along a continuum that relates to their degree of *insight orientation*. In some groups there is a great deal of emphasis placed on the ability of the members to reflect on their own behavior, feelings, and motivations and to understand why they behave and feel the way they do. In other groups, the emphasis is on accomplishing the stated objectives—for example completing the task, socializing, or changing a specific behavior—with little or no concern for member insight. When insight is considered to be an important element within the group, group members are usually selected for their ability to reflect their own behavior and feelings and for their ability to use words to understand and discuss this process with others.

The attainment of insight as a desirable outcome is related to the theoretical and value orientation of the therapist and the group. The more psychoanalytically oriented schools of psychotherapy place more emphasis on clients achieving insight into the meaning and origins of their problems. On the other end of the continuum, operant learning theory or behavior modification groups value behavior change. Other theoretical frameworks, such as transactional analysis, combine both insight and behavior change in their objectives. It is not the purpose here to answer the debate regarding the ultimate value of insight without behavior change or vice versa. The reader should simply be aware that degree of insight orientation is a continuum along which groups can be placed.

The final group structure parameter is that of *physical variables*. The time and place of group sessions, the number of therapists and clients in the group, and the length of group meetings are all important physical structure variables for describing the group. The actual physical structure of the group is closely related to the considerations of group objectives, types of clients, degree of structure, level of prevention, and the insight and theoretical orientation of the group. A task group may need a meeting room with a table on which to work, while a learning group may need a room with blackboard and chairs that can be moved around to provide practice space. Learning groups tend to meet for 1- to 3-hour periods to maximize learning, while psychotherapy groups may meet from 1 to 4 hours and sensitivity–encounter groups may meet from 3 hours to an entire weekend to accomplish their objectives.

None of these structural parameters will give an entire picture of what is occurring in the group. They are used at times, however, to describe the differences between groups, e.g., "This is an unstructured, insight-oriented group and the other group is more structured." Such a limited statement still does not describe the objectives of the group and what client needs it is designed to meet.

These first two group descriptors, objectives and structure, influence group process and group outcomes (see the chart below). Group process and group outcomes are discussed within the context of this model. Much more detailed discussions of group structure (Section II), group process (Section III), and group outcomes (Section IV) are presented later.

Objectives	→	*Structure*	→	*Process*	→	*Outcomes*
Support		Type of clients				
Task accomplishment		Level of prevention				
Socialization		Degree of structure				
Learning–behavior change		Theoretical orientation				
Human relations training		Insight orientation				
Psychotherapy		Physical variables				

GROUP PROCESS

Groups can also be described and defined in terms of their internal process. Once the objectives and the structure of the group are determined, the group leader can begin to consider the much more elusive variable of group process. How do people change in groups? What is it that occurs in groups that makes a difference? These questions are discussed as assessment issues that nurses must consider in their appraisal of actual or proposed health care groups. (The issue of curative factors is also presented in Section III in the consideration of intervention strategies that can be utilized by the group leader.)

The process of what occurs in small groups has been explored from several perspectives. Research on group dynamics has described groups in terms of their leadership, membership, goals, norms, and interaction of group members. Group therapists, on the other hand, have described the process of their groups in terms of insight, interpersonal learning, catharsis, and corrective emotional experience. Since the focus of this book is on health care groups, it is assumed that any group presented—whether support, task, or psychotherapy—will have an overall therapeutic objective. That is, the reason for conducting the group or referring the client to the group will be to meet a specific health care need. Therefore, the group process variables presented in the group treatment literature as curative factors will be given primary consideration in this discussion.

In 1955 Corsini and Rosenberg[1] abstracted three hundred group therapy articles and developed nine major categories of curative factors from those presented in the literature. While these categories represent only the published views of group therapists, they are worthy of mention. The nine categories are: acceptance, universalization, reality testing, altrusim, transference, spectator therapy, interaction, intellectualization, and ventilation.

What is most interesting about these categories of curative factors is that they have been substantiated in subsequent studies and found to be useful by both clients and therapists. There is a great deal of overlap between these categories and those reported in Berzon, Pious, and Parson's[2] study examining the views of patients in short-term, outpatient therapy groups. In Lieberman, Yalom, and Miles'[3] extensive study of 10 different types of encounter groups with nonpatients, again the clients and group leaders ranked a similar set of curative factors as being important.

Yalom, Tinklenberg, and Gilula[4] also studied the question of curative factors by interviewing and testing 20 long-term group therapy patients identified as being the "most successful patients" by their respective therapists. The findings of these studies combined with his own professional experience resulted in the following list of curative factors presented by Yalom:[5]

1. Instillation of hope
2. Universality
3. Imparting of information
4. Altruism
5. The corrective recapitulation of the primary family group
6. Development of socializing techniques
7. Imitative behavior
8. Interpersonal learning
9. Group cohesiveness
10. Catharsis
11. Existential factors

While Yalom admits that the distinctions between these categories are to some degree arbitrary, clients and therapists alike have been able to identify significant events during the course of their groups that correspond with these categories. One can also debate whether these factors are "mechanisms of change" or "conditions for change"; however, it is clear that all of them are a part of the ongoing process of various groups. It is my opinion that what Yalom describes as the curative factors in group therapy provide a substantial base for the discussion and classification of the therapeutic process within health care groups.

Instillation of hope is an important element in any type of therapeutic relationship. Often it is hope of cure or hope that things can be different that keeps the client returning for appointments. Some clients will even endure prolonged pain or emotional discomfort because of their hope for relief. The same holds true for health care groups.

In a group setting, the instillation of hope can be approached even more directly. No matter what the nature of the group, it is a common occurrence to find that other group members have experienced a similar feeling or event and lived through it. For example, in an ongoing group of postoperative clients one woman who had just undergone a radical mastectomy was able to talk directly with others who had experienced the same change in body image and fear of cancer she was experiencing and learn how they had worked through their feelings. The degree of hope that this type of sharing engenders should not be overlooked. During the initial stages of a group experience, hope that "because others have been able to endure or change perhaps I can too" may be all that a client has for comfort.

Several studies reported by Goldstein speak to the therapeutic effects of positive client and therapist expectations prior to treatment. It is important that the group leader communicate to new clients the belief that participation in the group will be beneficial. Organizations such as Recovery Incorporated and Alcoholics Anonymous rely heavily on the instillation of hope through the use of testimonials given by "cured" or "recovered" members at each group session. Syanon makes use of a similar phenomenon by utilizing ex-addicts as group leaders.

Universality is closely related to instillation of hope. As group members share their common experiences, they learn that they are not alone. They find that regardless of race, sex, occupation, or any other distinguishing personal attributes, the event or feeling they are experiencing is similar to that of some other human being. They learn that they are not so unique that their problems are beyond solution.

Many persons in today's society bear the weight of feelings of shame or inadequacy silently and alone. It is a welcome relief to unload this burden and find that others in the group are open and responsive to sharing a common experience. I have led groups in which a young woman reluctantly yet eagerly told the secret horrors of paternal rape that she previously felt too shameful to share. Invariably there is at least one other woman in the group who was subjected to either incest or the traumas of childhood enemas, which were a more rational, yet equally frightening, substitute. To find that one is not alone—that the carefully guarded secrets of being human are shared—is indeed a healing experience in and of itself.

The *imparting of information* includes all of the health care teaching that is done by the nurse and other group members. Whether or not it is the primary objective of the group, there is a considerable amount of information shared during the course of a health care group. Normal growth and development, normal and therapeutic diets, good physical and mental health practices, and the various stages in the grieving process are only a few types of information that can be learned in a group.

While cognitive information may be a necessary precondition for behavior change, in most instances knowledge alone is not enough to alter a client's health related behaviors. The nursing literature contains numerous examples of studies in which teaching the client about a low sodium diet had little or no lasting effect on dietary habits. As I was thinking about this section prior to writing it, I made the interesting mental slip of referring to the heading as "the implanting of information." Actually, many health professionals do approach client teaching as if it were a simple procedure of implanting information from one head into another. They are then surprised when the recipient rejects the donor information because it was not adapted or appropriate to the client's particular needs and situation.

Very few people will change with just information alone. On the other hand, there is a cognitive element that precedes behavioral change in most health care situations. The renal client must know his diet before he and the nurse can look together at why he is experiencing difficulty in following it. When information about physical and mental health practices is shared in a group, there is often benefit to more clients than just the one who asked the question. Perhaps there is also some secondary benefit in the process of sharing and experiencing others' willingness to share information.

The nurse should be cautioned, however, about the client who appears to be actively engaged in the group through his numerous requests for information. Closer scrutiny of the situation may reveal a person who receives a great deal of group attention by asking questions, but then fails to implement the information he has received. Another symptom of resistance to change is the client who asks for information and then engages the other group members in a frustrating series of "Yes, that's a good idea, but . . ." response. In this example, the person is also very successfully avoiding personal change.

Now that some of the problems with merely imparting information have been outlined, it is important to present some of the potential benefits of planning for a cognitive component in health care groups. Yalom et al[7] have demonstrated that clients who are provided information regarding the group structure, process, and feelings they might experience in the group are more active participants (measured in sessions two and twelve) than those members who met with the therapist for a standard history-taking session prior to entering the group. Perhaps the content of Yalom's preparation session provides clients with a cognitive structure of explaining and understanding what they are going to be experiencing.

As a clinician, I have often noted the considerable relief experienced by clients who have been told that anger is a normal part of the grieving process or that the confusion they are experiencing relative to giving up an old way of relating to people has been reported by others in a similar situation. Their own experience becomes more understandable and acceptable.

Johnson's[8] studies further demonstrate the value of imparting information regarding sensations as a method of reducing anxiety during a threatening event. Johnson's series of studies provide significant evidence that, prior to a traumatic, physical procedure, information about the procedure does not reduce emotional response during the procedure as much as information about what the client will be physically experiencing. This latter information reduces the client's fear of the unknown and makes the experience more predictable and understandable.

Both the Yalom et al and Johnson studies discuss the importance of helping the client to anticipate what he will be experiencing. While Yalom et al have not controlled for the effect of this variable, it is present in their orientation of clients for group psychotherapy. It would be interesting to explore the relative merits of having other clients in the group devote a portion of the group session to providing this orientation to new members. If experience level information itself is useful (and it seems to be), the sharing of this information by persons who have or who are experiencing it might increase the benefit to the new client and the group.

Altruism is the experience of sharing a part of oneself with others. Within a group setting there is opportunity for a great deal of sharing of information, support, feelings, experiences, and concrete assistance. If the group is cohesive and the members care about each other, it is not uncommon for group members to offer to call each other, visit, or share material goods to assist another member through a period of crisis or need.

Groups such as Alcoholics Anonymous or Recovery Inc. are based on the principle that there is therapeutic benefit in this process of clients helping each other. The development of colostomy, mastectomy, or amputee organizations in some communities is further evidence of the need for and benefit of helping persons who are in a similar situation to oneself. Very often a client's own recovery is facilitated when he finds a meaningful answer to the question, "What do I have to offer anyone else?"

Part of the socialization of clients to a health care group may involve providing evidence that clients can indeed help each other. The prevailing norm in our society is to expect individual service—prefereably from a physician—when dealing with a health care problem. Some clients doubt that other persons in a smiliar situation can help them and may regard groups as a second-rate form of assistance. The group leader needs to be convinced about the benefits of group intervention so that the client is given a clear and convincing message before entering the group. Once having experienced the support and assistance of the other group members, most clients readily shed their initial concerns about the group.

Groups can provide a *corrective recapitulation of the primary family group*. Because groups are composed of other members who can be symbolically viewed as siblings and a leader or leaders who can be viewed as more nurturing, expert, and powerful parent figures, clients are able to act out some of the conflicts they experienced in their primary family group. When group members dominate the conversation, sit quietly unless they are asked a question, set up arguments with the leader or other group members, or present themselves as being helpless, they are probably demonstrating behaviors that were learned and reinforced in their primary family. This is a general type of transference that all of us bring into our current relationships to some degree.

Since the composition of the group is such that it fosters these primary family behaviors, the group is also a setting in which clients can alter their previously learned responses. The leader and the group members can facilitate this change by acknowledging the client's behavior and responding to it differently than the family did. For example, the client who constantly dominates the group discussion can be helped to see that he is more likely to get his needs met by being clear and direct about what he wants. There is indeed enough help to go around, and his fear of being alone and helpless if he is not the center of attention is unfounded in the group.

Different groups will utilize this recapitulation of the primary family experience to varying degrees. In a task or learning group very little attention may be paid to the genetic origins of each member's behavior. A human relations training group may focus on the here and now effects of the member's behavior and assist him to alter it to elicit a different response from other people. In some psychotherapy groups, a great deal of time and attention is paid to understanding why the person is behaving and feeling the way he is. In other psychotherapy groups, the behavior itself may be the focus of attention with little concern about its origins. The one common therapeutic benefit, regardless of the nature of the group, appears to reside in the corrective nature of the leader and member responses to the behavior in question. If the client receives a more healthy response from the group than he did from his family, eventually the probability is greater that he will alter his behavior.

The *development of socializing techniques* is a process that is present to one degree or another in all health care groups. The degree to which relating to other people is an explicit part of the treatment contract may vary from one group to another. For example, an aftercare group for newly discharged state hospital patients may focus primarily on the development of social skills required for re-entry into the community. On the other hand, a support group or a psychotherapy group may not focus directly on developing social skills. These skills may occur as a secondary benefit of relating directly, honestly, and intimately to other people in the group.

For many people a health care group provides a unique opportunity to reflect on themselves and their relationships. The skills that are acquired in this type of atmosphere can be transferred into other intimate or social relationships. For example, a young mother who learns to be assertive about her own health care needs in her diabetic group is likely to respond differently to her friends and family when they are pressing her to engage in strenuous activity. She has learned that it is acceptable to take care of herself as well as to care about others and to consider the effects of her behavior on both herself and her friends and family.

The capacity for *imitative behavior* is developed at a very early age. Small children imitate the behavior of those who care for them and are rewarded for learning to talk and developing motor skills and appropriate interpersonal behavior. In later life persons still learn by imitation without necessarily being consciously aware of it.

In health care groups the other members as well as the leader become models of new, healthier behavior. The language and health care value system of the group are learned in part by imitation just as a child first learns to speak. The new behavior may at first seem awkward and not fully belonging to the person, but imitation may very well be the first step toward internalizing new behavior and values. There are many clients whose initial decisions to give up suicidal behavior were based on the value system of the therapist and the group. Later these people gradually internalized the feeling that their life is worth living.

Interpersonal learning is a complex process that overlaps several of the process variables already mentioned. Especially in psychotherapy and counselling groups, the process of interpersonal learning is utilized as one of the primary curative factors. Since most mental health problems are acquired interpersonally and are manifested in disturbed interpersonal relationships, it is reasonable that their treatment should focus on interpersonal learning.

The psychotherapy group provides an excellent medium in which the clients' various interpersonal styles can be readily displayed, explored, and corrected. In time, the group actually becomes a social microcosm in which the clients engage in a range of interpersonal behaviors that closely parallel their lives outside the group. It is a common group experience for the members to identify in the group the interpersonal problem for which a client is seeking help in his work, social, or home situation. For example, Cheryl, a bright, assertive, divorced woman with two young children was having difficulties in finding and maintaining adult companionship. She seemed genuinely confused when her attempts at friendship and intimacy resulted in a reserved and distant response from both men and women with whom she was attempting to establish contact. She would then withdraw and sulk, concluding that she was forever doomed to a life of lonely isolation and caring for her children. The group members were able to point out to Cheryl the similarities between what she was describing in her life and what had occurred within the group. They shared with her their fear of and withdrawal from Cheryl's seemingly desperate approaches for friendship. Indeed, Cheryl presented herself as such a needy person that others became frightened at what might be required of them in the relationship. The group provided a safe and unique forum in which Cheryl could receive this constructive feedback.

The use that is made of such interpersonal feedback depends to a large degree on the individual readiness of the client to change as well as on the level at which the group is functioning. Some people will change with just confrontation alone. In Cheryl's case, her feelings of isolation and loneliness had been acquired at a very early age and she had adopted a general "poor me" attitude in reacting to the world. The group format was one that allowed Cheryl to work on the origins of her interpersonal style. Eventually she was helped to see how her early attitudes about herself and her relationships with others had been influencing her current life situation. The group assisted Cheryl in taking a more objective look at her relationships and sorting out what was real and what was her own distortion of how others felt about her. It was with no small degree of shock and sadness that she arrived at the realization that she herself was setting up what she experienced as rejection from other people by the desperate manner in which she approached them.

Once the clients assume responsibility for the roles they are playing in creating their own interpersonal dilemma and understand the sequence of events that lead to their own dissatisfaction, the road is paved for behavioral change. Cheryl very quickly began to identify her own interpersonal responses, both inside and outside the group, that led to her feelings of isolation and loneliness. She received support from the therapist and group members that she was indeed an enjoyable person to be with when she was relating in the here and now and not anticipating rejection. As Cheryl practiced her new interpersonal style in the group, she was also able to give up her very early decision that she was a poor, helpless person, subject to the acceptance or rejection of other people. She experienced for herself the advantages of approaching relationships from a position of strength rather than weakness.

Of course the process of interpersonal learning outlined in Cheryl's case occurs over a period of time. Concurrently, other group members are also working on similar issues for themselves and with each other. The point to be emphasized is that within a psychotherapy group many persons experience this constructive interpersonal feedback and corrective emotional experience for the first time. In social relationship situations people are much less likely to take the time and care involved in giving someone clear, direct feedback. In the group, however, a skilled therapist is able to make use of the presence of other people to provide not only for the clear, direct feedback, but for a therapeutic process of interpersonal learning and an outcome of interpersonal change.

Group cohesiveness is not only a process variable, but a necessary condition for the therapeutic functioning and outcomes of most, if not all, health care groups. Yalom[5] describes cohesiveness in group therapy as being the analogue of the relationship in individual therapy. They also say that group cohesiveness is a broad concept, "encompassing the patient's relationship to the group therapist, to the other group members, and to the group as a whole."

In the group dynamics literature, Festinger[9] defines the forces that a group can exert on its members as cohesiveness: "the resultant of all forces acting on the members to remain in the group." What appears important from the two preceding definitions is the value that both place on the bond or attraction that occurs between and among group members and leader(s). The result of this attraction can be equated to a magnetic field that holds the group together and thus sets the stage for working within the group.

It might be useful at this point to repeat the definition of the term "group" as it is being used in this text. Of the multitude of definitions available, I have found Lewin's[10] concept of a group as being "a dynamic whole based on interdependence rather than similarity" to be a useful definition to apply to health care groups. In this context, a collection of persons on the same hospital ward are not necessarily a group even though they share a similar condition. They become a group when they are in some way interdependent for some aspect of their physical or emotional functioning.

The element of interdependence is essential to understanding group cohesiveness. For example, the above collection of hospitalized persons may become a group by deciding to eat their meals together in the dayroom or to watch the World Series together. To the extent that they have decided to rely on each other for social contact and the sharing of a common experience, they have become a group. Whether or not they accomplish their objective will depend on the degree of group cohesiveness.

A number of group therapy studies illustrate the importance of group cohesiveness.[3,4,11-14] The most common conclusion of these studies is that attraction to the group and the quality of member to member interaction is a strong determinant of positive therapeutic outcome in the clients and groups studied. Group cohesiveness can affect the attendance rate, the quality and quantity of member interaction, and the influence that members have on each other.

More specific attention will be given to the ways in which the leader can influence group cohesiveness in Chapter 7. At this point it is important, however, to emphasize the influence that this particular process variable can have on group outcomes. It stands to reason that persons who are attracted to the goals and norms of the group will attend group sessions and will be more likely to follow the health care prescriptions of the members and leader. Group cohesiveness is therefore an important method for capturing the attention and commitment of clients in the process of influencing their health behaviors.

Catharsis is a process variable that is cited by many group therapy clients as being an important aspect of their group experience. The expression of emotions previously unexpressed has long been considered of therapeutic value by psychotherapists. However, very few experienced therapists believe that catharsis alone is sufficient to produce long-standing therapeutic change. If anger, sadness, fear, or pleasure are expressed, they must also be integrated into the ongoing experience of the client.

Research on the outcomes and process of group psychotherapy and encounter groups conducted by Lieberman, Yalom, and Miles[3] and by Yalom, Tinklenberg, and Gilula[4] support the interrelatedness of catharsis with other group process variables. Merely "getting things off my chest" was not rated by clients as being nearly as important as items such as "learning to express my feelings." The results of these studies indicate that catharsis, or expression of feelings, must occur within the context of interpersonal relatedness and in concert with cognitive learning. Thus, the client who expresses anger directly toward another group member is more likely to benefit from this experience if the group provides a safe environment in which these feelings can be expressed and worked through and if the therapist is able to help the individual client and group to learn from the experience.

Catharsis is also related to group cohesiveness in a circular cause-and-effect fashion. The expression and mutual working through of strong emotions is likely to increase the feelings of closeness and cohesiveness of the group. On the other hand group cohesiveness is a necessary prerequisite for group members to share their feelings. This is the reason there is so little sharing of strong emotions during the early phases of a treatment group.

The objectives of the group will also exert a strong influence over the use of catharsis as a group process variable. A group whose objective is socialization may be less tolerant of the expression of feelings that are perceived as interfering with having a good time. A task group may define assisting members with feelings as being outside their objectives. Feelings may be dealt with in a learning group only insofar as they interfere with the learning objectives of the group. It is primarily in human relations training and psychotherapy groups that catharsis is viewed as contributing directly to achieving the objectives of the group.

Existential factors are those elements in the process of a group that help members to deal with the meaning of their own existence. These existential factors are more likely to be present in a group that is concerned with thinking, talking, and feeling rather than in a group whose focus is doing something.

When people come together and share the experience of having a terminal illness, the experience of divorce, or the experience of feeling scared or angry, there is a certain comfort to be found in the sharing and commonality of one's experience. There is also a sobering solitude when one confronts the reality that they alone must decide to change. Whether the experience is one of deciding how to confront life or how to deal with death, each person is at once a part of yet separate from all other persons in their environment. A group that is open to acknowledging this fact can utilize such existential factors in helping its members to live their lives differently because of this awareness.

In summary, the eleven group process variables described above are important factors to consider in the assessment of groups. They help to explain how people change in groups and offer ways through which the group leader or therapist can utilize the group process to therapeutic advantage. As has been stated, not all of these process variables are present or present to the same degree in every group. Also, different process variables are important at different stages in the life of the group.

GROUP OUTCOMES

Finally, groups can be defined and described in terms of their outcomes. While the outcomes of any health care group experience should be related to the initial objectives and client needs for the group, the actual evaluation of outcomes is usually more extensive than the statement of objectives. To give a complete overview of the variables involved in assessing groups, an introduction to the group outcome variables, which will be discussed more thoroughly in Section IV, is presented here. While this may appear to be a bit out of sequence, the assessment of group objectives, structure, and process is incomplete without the consideration of group outcomes.

In their simplest form, the outcomes of health care groups are no different than the outcomes of any other therapeutic intervention—the clients either benefit or they do not. There are numerous methods that have been used to define the benefits of nursing interventions, but only recently have nurse researchers begun to focus more specifically on outcome measures. If something beneficial has transpired during the therapeutic process, it should be reflected in a beneficial outcome.

For some clients the major outcome of the health care group experience is *maintenance*. Maintenance of emotional and/or behavioral status is a very significant outcome for certain types of clients who enter the group with a high probability of becoming worse and with very little chance of improvement. Some aftercare groups are comprised of members for whom the major objective and most exciting outcome is to maintain their current level of functioning and to prevent rehospitalization. This means that their emotional and behavioral strengths must be supported, and the group leader needs to be realistic in not expecting to "cure" the group. Socialization groups and support groups both place a great deal of emphasis on maintenance of existing emotional and behavioral strengths.

Another general outcome of the group experience is *learning*. The acquisition of knowledge or information is often essential in groups dealing with health care issues. While learning is not equated with a change in client behavior, within this context it is regarded as a prerequisite to certain types of behavior change. Clients can be presented with information about medication, dietary, and life-style changes they will need to make. They can then be tested for their acquisition and/or retention of this information. The outcome at this point is merely whether or not they learned the information. When such health care information is presented in a group, it is important to develop outcome measures that will provide information about the learning of individuals within the group.

Groups can also assist clients to learn about themselves and their relationships with other people. Yalom[5] describes four types of insight, or learning, about oneself that can occur in the therapeutic group process. First, clients may learn how they are seen by other people. They may receive feedback on how they appear angry, seductive, aloof, depressed, or uncaring. Secondly, clients may learn what they are doing to and with other people. This understanding of what they are doing in relationships requires a perspective of the cumulative effect of their interactional style and the interpersonal consequences of their behaviors. For example, a woman who appears weak and helpless and hides her own capabilities from the men she meets needs to see the connection between her own behavior and her inability to establish a satisfying relationship with a man who respects her.

Thirdly, clients may learn why they do what they do to themselves and other people. This "motivational insight" would assist the woman in the above example to learn that her weak and helpless approach to people, especially men, is based on a fear of becoming aggressive and perhaps angry. The fourth level of insight, which Yalom calls "genetic insight," involves helping clients learn how they got to be the way they are. Depending on the therapist's theoretical orientation, genetic insight may or may not be necessary to the process of learning and behavior change.

Learning about oneself and one's relationships with other people can occur in a variety of types of groups. Another outcome that is often closely related to interpersonal learning is learning about how to change. While some group leaders or therapists assume that information about how clients relate is sufficient to help them to change, other leaders focus much more deliberately and specifically on helping clients learn how to change. In these groups considerable time and attention may be focused on the process of changing clients' feelings about themselves, how to relate differently with other people, and specifically how to alter one's personal environment. From my experience, there is a fairly large group of clients who need to learn how to change in addition to learning what to change.

As was pointed out earlier, the learning of information does not always or necessarily result in behavior change. *Behavior change*, therefore, needs to be viewed as a distinct outcome. Even in the most clearly defined and structured group experience, therapists and group leaders are often surprised at the actual changes made by their clients. It is not uncommon for a client to casually report a significant decision such as enrolling in school or making a positive job change as a result of what was happening in the group. This type of occurrence makes the job of assessing group outcomes a bit more difficult, since it is not always clear what client changes were a direct or indirect result of the group experience.

Generally speaking, client behavior changes can be categorized as changes in self, changes in interpersonal relationships, and changes in personal environment. In changing themselves, clients may change their own behavior, e.g., becoming more physically active and improving their diet, and/or they may change how they feel about themselves, e.g., deciding to be "physically attractive" rather than "fat and lazy." This self-concept change very often occurs together with the related behavioral change.

When clients change the style or quality of their interpersonal relationships, the difference is often quite noticeable in their relationships within the group. In fact, the group may serve as a practice setting for working out a new style of relating. Clients may become more assertive, decide to be specific about what they want from other people, stop being afraid that others will not like them, or listen more closely to what others are saying. Most groups value and provide support for the client to generalize these new interpersonal skills to relationships outside the group.

Another major outcome of health care groups is change in the client's personal environment. These changes may range from reorganizing the kitchen to facilitate food preparation for an older person, to deciding to change jobs and move to a new location, or to deciding to find a roommate. Whatever the environmental change, it is often the result of group discussions about ways of maintaining or improving the physical and/or mental health status of the client. Many physical and mental health problems can be solved by assisting the clients to alter their personal physical environments.

A MODEL FOR GROUP ASSESSMENT

We have discussed many ideas in developing an assessment model for the small group variables of objectives, structure, process, and outcomes. These are four very important and interrelated components in assessing small groups. As I have stated previously, their interrelatedness can be demonstrated in the following manner:

Objectives → Structure → Process → Outcomes

The difficulties of categorizing the different types of groups and defining what occurs in them has already been discussed. In the process of developing the above model, I have become increasingly aware of the complexities of group as opposed to individual interventions. As with most models, the one above does not account for all the variance that can occur in the real world. It does, however, give beginning clinicians a place to start in attempting to make sense out of the real world of their own practices.

The model begins with group objectives, which have hopefully been determined by prior assessment of client need. It then proposes that clearly stated objectives plus clear decisions regarding the various structural components of the group will result in a certain group process that will yield certain group outcomes. This model will be developed in much more detail in subsequent chapters.

At this point, there are several aspects of the model that can be applied to the assessment of small group variables. Consider the following chart that was developed in an attempt to display the interrelatedness between objectives for the various general types of groups, the process one would generally expect to occur in those groups, and the types of outcome both client and nurse could expect. The six general categories of group objectives are those presented earlier in this chapter. I have attempted to check the group process variables that are most likely to be emphasized in each type of group. On this chart the double checks (✓✓) indicate the most important process variable(s) for each type of group. This type of process chart can also

Table 1

Objectives		Psychotherapy	Human relations	Learning	Socialization	Task	Support
Process	Instillation of hope	✔		✔			✔
	Universality	✔	✔	✔	✔		✔
	Imparting information	✔	✔	✔✔		✔	✔
	Altruism	✔	✔	✔	✔		✔
	Corrective family group	✔					
	Devel. socializing techniques	✔			✔✔		
	Imitative behavior	✔	✔	✔			
	Interpersonal learning	✔✔	✔✔				✔
	Group cohesiveness	✔	✔	✔	✔	✔	✔✔
	Catharsis	✔					
	Existential factors	✔					
	Task orientation			✔		✔✔	
Outcomes	Maintenance	Lo	Lo	Lo	Hi	Lo	Hi
	Learning	Med	Hi	Hi	Lo	Med	Med
	Behavior change	Hi	Med	Hi	Lo	Med	Lo

be completed by the nurse in assessing the process of any other specific group in the health care setting. Since many health care groups have a combination of objectives, a slightly different set of process variables may emerge as the process of each group is assessed.

Likewise, in assessing outcomes one can assign different ratings to maintenance, learning, and behavior change in assessing any health care group. The high (Hi), medium (Med), and low (Lo) ratings assigned to the outcome variables for each type of group is my attempt to state a weighting for the relative importance of each outcome to the general group objectives. Again, as the nurse assesses health care groups with mixed objectives, these ratings may very well be different. For example, a support group that utilizes tasks such as planning a group brunch to structure its activities will make use of the process variables of both the support and task group categories. In fact, the support variables will probably be weighted more heavily than those required to accomplish the task of organizing and putting on a brunch. The expected outcomes will be heavily weighted toward maintenance with a moderate emphasis on learning and behavior change. The weighting of learning and behavior change will depend largely on whether the group members already have the knowledge and skills required to accomplish the task.

In summary, the assessment of small group variables is a complex undertaking. The nurse dealing with health care groups is encouraged to be as clear and specific as possible in the assessment of objectives, structure, process, and outcomes. This initial precision is urged because actual groups are never that precise. Any initial confusion will only become compounded when the nurse later attempts to deal with the interrelatedness between objectives, structure, process, and outcomes. Just as members affect each other within the group, these assessment variables also affect each other. With this assessment foundation in place, the clinician can now proceed with the task of structuring, processing, and evaluating health care groups.

REFERENCES

1. Corsini, R., and Rosenberg, B.: Mechanisms of group psychotherapy: Processes and dynamics, J. Abnorm. Soc. Psychol. **51**:406-411, 1955.
2. Berzon, B., Pious, C., and Parson, R.: The therapeutic event in group psychotherapy: A study of subjective reports by group members, J. Individ. Psychol. **19**:204-212, 1963.
3. Lieberman, M. A., Yalom, I. D., and Miles, M. B.: Encounter groups: First facts, New York, 1972, Basic Books, Inc.
4. Yalom, I. D., Tinklenberg, J., and Gilula, M.: Curative factors in group therapy, unpublished study.
5. Yalom, I. D.: The theory and practice of group psychotherapy, New York, 1975, Basic Books, Inc.
6. Goldstein, A. P.: Therapist patient expectancies in psychotherapy, New York, 1962, Pergamon Press.
7. Yalom, I. D., Houts, P. S., Newell, G., and Rand, K. H.: Preparation of patients for group therapy, Arch. Gen. Psychiatry **17**:416-427, 1967.

8. Johnson, J.: Stress reduction through sensation information. In Sarason, I. G., and Spielberger, C. D. (eds.): Stress and anxiety, vol. 2, Washington D.C., in press, Hemisphere Publishing Co.

9. Festinger, L.: Informal social communication. In Cartwright, D., and Zander, A. (eds.): Group dynamics, New York, 1968, Harper & Row, Publishers, p. 185.

10. Lewin, K.: Resolving social conflicts, New York, 1948, Harper & Row, Publishers, p. 184.

11. Dickoff, H., and Lakin, M.: Patient's views of group psychotherapy: Retrospections and interpretations, Int. Group Psychother. 13:61-73, 1963.

12. Kapp, F. T., et al.: Group participation and self-perceived personality change, J. Nerv. Ment. Dis. 139:255-265, 1964.

13. Yalom, I. D., Houts, P. S., Zimerberg, S. M., and Rand, K. H.: Prediction of improvement in group therapy, Arch. Gen. Psychiatry 17:159-168, 1967.

14. Clark, J. B., and Culbert, S. A.: Mutual therapeutic perception and self-awareness in a T-group, J. Appl. Behav. Sci. 1:180-194, 1965.

Section II

Intervention— small group structure

This section is written with the assumption that the nurse will be functioning in the role of leader for a group of clients. The general, underlying objective of the group will be either the promotion, maintenance, or restoration of the biopsychosocial functioning of the clients. In the broadest sense, we will be referring to health care groups that may take a variety of forms depending on the needs of the clients, the objectives and preparation of the nurse, and the treatment expectations of the health care system in which the clients and nurse are engaged.

The model for establishing a health care group in Fig. 1 is the result of

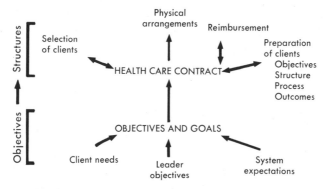

Fig. 1
Model of small group variables—objectives and structures.

the discussion of the assessment of small group objectives in Section I. The variables in this model are presented in this section as factors that must be considered in setting up a health care group. Since there are very few right or wrong ways to go about structuring a group, the relative advantages and disadvantages of different group structures will be discussed. Whenever relevant clinical or group dynamics research exists, the implications of these studies will also be presented.

The general intent of this section is to prepare nurse-clinicians to make reasonable decisions about the structure of health care groups within their clinical practice. We will examine the treatment contract as a function of the selection of clients, the development of mutual expectations, and the physical arrangements, reimbursement, and preparation of clients.

4 □ Selection of clients

The dilemma of where to begin in organizing a health care group is a very real one. Very few clients approach the nurse requesting a group in which they can learn about the life-style changes following coronary artery bypass surgery or the social skills required upon discharge from a state hospital. If some clients know to ask for emotional counselling, very few are sophisticated enough to ask for group counselling sessions. The initial assessment of client needs that can best be met in a group as presented in Section I is very often the responsibility of the nurse. Because of their ongoing contact with clients and their families, it is usually the nurses who are in a position to make the suggestion that a group intervention would be desirable.

Frequently, nurses realize that a number of clients in their care or with whom they have contact are demonstrating a similar need or problem. The nurse may notice that most of the returning young veterans are suffering from a similar social isolation in addition to their health care problems, that a large number of hypertensive outpatients abandon their dietary and medication prescriptions after about 2 months in the clinic, or that mothers of high-risk infants seem to have difficulty caring for their babies once they are well enough to be taken home.

Even patients who do not share a common diagnostic problem may share similar needs that could be met in a group. This may be especially true on a general medical-surgical hospital unit where many patients would benefit from an opportunity to discuss their concerns about being ill and away from their families. This heterogeneity of group composition may also be true in a public health nurse's case load where a number of clients who need emotional support could benefit from a group.

The model in Fig. 1 demonstrates the way in which client needs, thera-

47

pist objectives, and system expectations converge to produce the objectives and goals for the group. These variables are discussed in more detail in Section I. The reason they are mentioned again in this chapter on selection of clients is that the objectives and goals for the group have a direct influence on the types of clients to be included in the group.

Let us proceed then with the assumption that the nurse's assessment of client needs, therapist objectives, and system expectations are all congruent and lead to the clear statement of objectives and goals that can be accomplished in a small group. If the assessment questions presented in Chapter 2 have been utilized, the nurse will already have developed the contents for a written proposal for a group intervention. It is my opinion that writing a proposal for the group is a very useful exercise. It can serve as a vehicle for assisting nurses in clarifying their own ideas and plans, and it is often a necessary step in obtaining administrative approval for the group. A good proposal for a group should include a complete assessment of client needs, an explanation of the relationship between client needs and group objectives, and a clear statement of anticipated outcomes. The group proposal on pp. 49 and 50 was submitted to the Director of Nursing by an evening charge nurse on a general medical-surgical unit in a large teaching hospital.

Some details of this proposal have been omitted. The primary purpose of the example is to demonstrate the type of congruence that must exist between client needs, group objectives, and anticipated outcomes and the effect this has on the selection of clients for the group.

It is important to remember that since the client needs have been identified and the group objectives have been determined in this illustration, the nurse will need to explain the various aspects of the group to the potential members. Some patients on the ward may not be experiencing a similar need or may be unwilling to participate in such a group. Still other patients may not be aware of feeling lonely in the evenings or have not considered an alternative to their isolation. In any event, the nurse will need to approach potential group members with a thorough explanation of the objectives and goals for the group.

In all groups, it is important to know who defined the client need and what is the source of referral. All too often a well-meaning family member or health care professional will refer the client for help without involving the client in the decision. The group leader should always take the time to determine what the client defines as his need and why he is coming for help. This point will be discussed in more detail when the preparation of clients for the group and the development of mutual expectations are considered.

To:

From:

Assessment of client
needs

I have been working permanent evenings on 7 West for the past 6 months. During this time I have observed the large number of patients who are referred to our hospital from distances of several hundred miles. These patients are frequently alone during visiting hours because their families are unable to make such a long trip to visit every evening. There are usually eight to twelve of these patients on our unit at any given time. As I have talked with these patients individually they seem to have a common feeling of loneliness as they watch the other patients whose families are visiting. They also express a need for some form of socialization between dinner and the time they go to sleep. They seem to be unaware that other patients are experiencing similar feelings and needs.

Group objectives and
goals

What I would like to do is form a voluntary group that would meet for 2 hours each evening between dinner and bedtime. One purpose of the group would be to provide emotional support for patients who are experiencing the loneliness of hospitalization and concern about their physical condition in the absence of their usual family or support system. The first 45 minutes of our group session would be devoted to a discussion of how the group participants feel about their physical condition and hospitalization. With some guidance from me, I think the group will be able not only to share feelings, but also to help each other determine alternative ways of dealing with their current situations.

Another purpose of the group would be to provide opportunities for socialization for these patients who do not have evening visitors. After the group discussion period, the patients will be encouraged to divide into small groups for card games, watching T.V., or using the various games, books, and projects provided by the volunteers. I have arranged for use of the sun porch, which is large enough for a variety of small group activities.

Anticipated outcomes   I would like to try out this evening group for a 3-month period and evaluate the results at the end of that time. I do not expect that the group will take any more—and perhaps less—of my time than talking with each of these patients individually during the course of the evening. The outcome I anticipate for the patients is that they will feel less lonely and isolated during their hospitalization. By sharing their feelings with each other and by doing some constructive problem solving, these patients should be able to maintain their previous levels of coping with their health care situations. Hopefully they can utilize the group as a substitute family during their hospitalization. Some group members may also learn new ways of coping through the sharing that will occur in the group. The primary outcome, however, is the maintenance of each patient's previous level of social skills and self-care potential regarding his health problem.

Any patients who are not expecting visitors on a particular evening will be asked if they want to participate in the group that evening. Only those patients who are unable to participate because of either being comatose or a critical physical condition will not be asked to join the group. The sun-room is large enough to accommodate patients in wheelchairs or on stretchers. Because of the objectives of the group and the type of patients on our ward, I expect that eight to twelve patients will participate each evening. There will be some continuity in membership, depending on who is having visitors and the usual admissions and discharges.

There has been much discussion but very little research on the criteria to be used in the selection of clients for groups. The nurse who is selecting clients for a group experience has two choices: who to include and who to exclude. The available research on psychotherapy groups suggests that it is perhaps easier to decide who to exclude than who to include in group treatment experiences. There is consensus among clinicians and researchers that persons who are brain damaged,[1,2] suicidal,[3,4] addicted to drugs or alcohol,[1,2] acutely psychotic,[4-6] or sociopathic[7] should be excluded from intensive, outpatient group psychotherapy. Of these types of clients, alcoholics, drug addicts, and sociopaths have been successfully treated in their own therapy groups. Brain-damaged, suicidal, and acutely psychotic persons generally require more individual treatment attention than is available in a group setting. Generally, the decision to recommend exclusion of these types of patients from psychotherapy groups has been based on studies concerned with group therapy "failures" or "dropouts." There are also some group therapists who believe that any of the above types of clients can be treated in groups along with persons who do not have the same problem. What does emerge from the literature is the conclusion that not all clients succeed in group forms of treatment. What is not so clear is the answer as to why. I believe that the explanation for group "failures" can be found in one or several of three dimensions: individual characteristics of the client, preferences or characteristics of the therapist, and/or factors inherent in the group.

Certain clients will not select or accept a group form of intervention. When presented with the availability of expectant parent classes, group therapy, or an aftercare group, they respond negatively and some remain unconvinced despite the stated advantages of the group. Once the nurse has provided the client with the information necessary to make a decision, the client's refusal should be respected. Often clients themselves are aware of the form of assistance they will best utilize. If a client wants individual health care attention, he is not likely to participate in the group to any therapeutic advantage regardless of the nurse's attempts at coercion.

As mentioned earlier, clients who require a great deal of individual attention and health care intervention are not likely candidates for groups. The overtly psychotic, suicidal, or brain-damaged persons referred to previously often exhibit a characteristic need for individual attention. Some of these persons can be helped initially through learning to relate to one person. Once the original crisis is over or the client has learned basic relationship and social skills, a group form of intervention might be considered beneficial.

Preferences or characteristics of the therapist that interact with client success in groups need to be considered. As helping persons, nurses are often expected to be all things to all people. This is absolutely not true—nor is it possible. All group leaders or therapists have types of clients with whom they enjoy working and with whom they are therefore likely to be more effective than with others. Some therapists enjoy listening while others want to be intervening much more actively. Some therapists are delighted by the energetic resistance of addicts while others feel much more comfortable in working with clients who have made a clear commitment to change their behavior. There is clearly an interaction between effectiveness and satisfaction on the part of the therapist that needs to be recognized. Therapists should be encouraged to become familiar with their own personal characteristics and preferences in the selection of clients. The success of clients is definitely affected by this factor.

Finally, factors that are inherent in the group itself can influence the success or failure of clients in group forms of intervention. By its very nature, a group requires that its members conform to certain expectations and participate in the defined group process. This participation usually necessitates a degree of interpersonal relatedness and ability and/or willingness to cooperate in accomplishing the group goal. A study conducted by Yalom et al explored the pretherapy factors that might be utilized to predict successful outcomes in therapy groups.

The results indicated that a large number of factors were *not* predictive of success in group therapy, including: level of psychological sophistication, the therapists' prediction of outcome, previous self-disclosure, and demographic data. In fact, the only variables predictive of success were the patient's attraction to the group and the patient's general popularity in the group (both measured at the sixth and twelfth meetings). The finding that popularity correlated highly with successful outcome has some implications for selection, because the researchers found that high previous self-disclosure, activity in the group and the ability to introspect were some of the prerequisites for group popularity.[8]

Since the above research was conducted on psychotherapy groups, the findings should not be generalized to other types of groups that nurses might conduct. The findings do, however, correlate with the group dynamics research that indicates that the type of member interaction correlates with group cohesiveness, which affects group productivity.[9] If one agrees with the assertion that cohesiveness is to group functioning what the relationship is to individual interactions, some tentative conclusions can be drawn regarding who will "succeed" and who will "fail" in health care groups. It can be hypothesized that group members who subscribe to the goals of the group and who are capable of and willing to adhere to the norms of the group will be effective, successful group members. There is a great need for clinical nursing research to explore this hypothesis.

If the above hypothesis is true, persons who are not committed to the goals of the group and capable of and committed to adhering to the norms of the group should be excluded from group membership. In this model, the exclusion criteria are exactly the opposite of the inclusion criteria. It is important to stress again that these ideas regarding the selection of clients need to be empirically tested.

I prefer to use a decision-making framework of who to include in health care groups (rather than who to exclude). If the objectives and goals for the proposed group are clear, the first inclusion variable is also clear. Does the client need coincide with the group objective? If the client need is socialization and the group objective is learning–behavior change, there will be dissonance between the client need and the group objectives. If the client need is weight loss and the group objective is supportive dietary control and weight reduction and maintenance, the client need and group objectives are compatible.

The next decision point relates to the extent to which the client subscribes to the objectives of the health care group. In other words, do the nurse's assessment of the client's needs and the client's perceptions of his needs coincide and is he willing to meet his needs in a health care group? A client who denies that he has any feelings or problems with returning to his former life-style after 2 years in Viet Nam is not likely to use a supportive or problem-solving group for returning veterans. In some settings such clients are pushed to join the group in the hope that the group contact will increase their awareness that they have a problem and do need help. The difficulty with this approach is that it distracts the group from its major objective. While the group is busy trying to convince one or two clients that they have problems for which they need help, they are not working on their primary objective of support and solving their own identified problems. The inclusion of a resistant member in a working group will deflect the group from its stated goals and objectives, thereby decreasing group cohesiveness and productivity.

I do have several suggestions for working with resistant clients. Sometimes the nurse or another client who has had a similar experience can work effectively on an individual basis to help the resistant client see his need to work on a given problem area. Once convinced, the client can join the group and become an effective group member. If a client remains unconvinced of his need, for whatever reason, his resistance should be respected. He should also be provided with information regarding how to obtain help should he ever decide he needs it.

The decision about the compatibility of client needs with group objectives and the degree to which the client is committed to doing something about his health care problem is not always an easy one. As group leaders, nurses must make the judgment based on their experience once they have obtained the necessary information. How much motivation to change is required before a client is a good candidate for inclusion in the group? How much compatibility of client needs and group objectives is desirable for the development of a cohesive group? We do not have concrete answers to these and similar questions. Even experienced group therapists are occasionally surprised when a client for whom they predicted a minimal level of group functioning becomes one of the most active and valuable group members. On the other hand, a client who initially appears to meet all of the therapist's criteria for inclusion in the group can become an early group dropout.

One important piece of information that can be used in making the decisions of whether or not to include a client in a health care group is the client's ability to adhere to the norms of the group. Norms are the standards of behavior—the spoken and unspoken rules—of the group. In one sense, norms are the methods the group uses to accomplish its objectives. As with the client's commitment to group goals, the degree of ability and commitment to adhere to the group norms will affect the cohesiveness and thereby the productivity of the group.

When forming new groups, nurses will have to rely on their own expectations of group behavior and their judgment of group norms that will be desirable once the group is established. When the nurse is adding clients to an established, ongoing group that has clearly developed norms, this judgment process is a bit easier. Potential clients can be asked if they are able and willing to attend every session, to call if they are unable to attend, to pay a set fee, to come on time, to read materials before each group session, or whatever other rules are established for participation in the group. If the objective of the group requires that members are able and willing to discuss their problems openly with others, will the client do this? If members are expected to do readings or adhere to a prescribed diet in a learning–behavior change group, will the client accept this as part of the contract for group membership? Is the client able to keep pace with other group members in the work of the group? It is best to know if the answer to any of these or other similar questions is no before placing the client in a specific group. No client needs the experience of failing or dropping out of a group experience because of a faulty selection procedure. No group needs the strain and distraction from its primary task that is caused by members entering and leaving the group unnecessarily.

With all of this advance warning about the careful selection of group members in accordance with the goals and norms of the group, it is important to add that very few tools exist to assist in making this decision. Some group therapists have found the FIRO-B (Fundamental Interpersonal Relations Orientation-Behavior)[10] self-administered questionnaire to be useful in predicting client behavior in groups. The FIRO-B system measures the person's needs for control, inclusion, and affection in constructing a profile of how he relates to other people.

Other group therapists have conducted research on the assumption that the best predictor of group behavior is previous behavior in a similar group.[11-13] Some have even established waiting room groups as a decision-making device in the selection of clients for different groups.[14] Even if nurses had time to develop such a group for the selection of group members, it is not clear that the results would produce any better selection of clients than would their own clinical judgment.

What does seem reasonable is that the nurse should obtain as much data as is practical and possible in selecting group members who will participate in and benefit from a group experience. One such category of information is previous group membership. The nurse should solicit information regarding groups of which the client is or has been a member. These can include work groups, treatment or health care groups, social clubs and groups, or other activities relevant to working and sharing with other people. The nurse should find out how the client became involved in the group, what role he played in the group, how he felt about his experience, and what benefits he realized from being in the group. This information will not give the nurse the final answer about inclusion in a specific health care group, but it will provide a larger, more relevant data base on which to make a decision.

There is a definite need for developing an empirical basis for the selection of clients for health care group experiences. The small amount of group psychotherapy research that is available cannot be directly applied to the health care groups that are part of nursing practice. Nurses need to conduct their own research to determine which clients do well in groups.

One final issue regarding the selection of clients for health care groups involves the actual grouping or assignment of clients to groups. What mix of clients will product the most therapeutic results? Again, the literature and research on therapy groups are inconclusive. There are as many arguments for homogeneous groups as for heterogeneous groups. There seems to be no inherent advantage in constructing a group in which all the members are similar or in which all the members are dissimilar. There is considerable latitude in deciding the right mix of clients for any particular group.

The real question for the clinician is, "Along what dimension should homogeneity or heterogeneity be determined?" Is age, sex, diagnosis, verbal skill, insight, degree of chronicity, or some other variable the most significant determinant of group composition? In my opinion the objectives, goals, and norms of the group that influence the selection of clients should also guide the therapist in the decisions regarding which clients should be assigned to which groups. For example, a group whose objective is to help hospitalized adolescents deal with their feelings about illness and their related changes in body image will be composed of hospitalized adolescents. It will not make any difference if each of the young people in the group has a different diagnosis. Nor will it matter if the members have been ill for different lengths of time, as long as they could benefit from working on the issues of illness and body image. The goal of this group might be to help the adolescents to become more accepting of their physical limitations and to determine ways in which they might modify their life-styles to compensate for their illnesses. Ideally then, the group would be composed of hospitalized adolescents who shared this goal. If the method of accomplishing this goal, or the group norms, included a willingness and ability to talk about their feelings and consider alternative solutions to their current situation, members would be grouped according to their facility with these norms.

It is a matter of clinical judgment exactly how much deviance with respect to the objectives, goals, and norms can be tolerated by any given group. At times, a group can accept a new member who is only moderately committed to the goals of the group and eventually help this member to change. I have led insight-oriented groups in which a nonverbal member was supported and nurtured until he was able to openly discuss his problems with the group. At other times, a person who deviates only slightly from the goals or norms of the group will be considered as extremely threatening by the other group members and they will close ranks to exclude this person.

I believe that this difference relates to the relative strength of the group goals and norms—how long they have been in effect and the degree to which group members are committed to them. A well-established group of ten members can tolerate one or two new members who challenge the goals or norms. A new group that is not yet certain of where it is going or how it will get there can usually tolerate very little deviance. Group deviants will be discussed in more detail as a group process issue in Section III. The major point to be made regarding group composition is that a fair degree of homogeneity regarding the objectives, goals, and norms of the group is desirable.

On the other hand, a group that is heterogeneous regarding other demographic characteristics—age, sex, diagnosis, and life-style—tends to provide a wider range of clinical material and enhances group functioning. The support and problem-solving group for hospitalized patients without visitors that was discussed earlier will benefit from a well-rounded group of old and young, male and female patients with a variety of physical problems. Each group member has something slightly different to learn from the others and something unique to contribute to the group. In one very meaningful exchange in such a group, an upper middle-class, successful business executive who was dying of cancer shared his conclusions about life, death, and money with a young student who was angry that his appendectomy had interfered with his A average in law school. The major commonality between these two men was their willingness to share their experiences. Beyond this commitment, they each learned and gained the most from their differences.

In summary, group members should be selected and grouped according to their commitment to the group objectives and goals and to their ability to participate in the group norms. Many group leaders find heterogeneity regarding other personal characteristics to be desirable. Research into the issues of selection and grouping of group members is required to convert this process from a clinical act into more of a clinical science with an empirical base for decision making.

REFERENCES

1. Nash, E., Frank, J., Gliedman, L., Imber, S., and Stone, A.: Some factors related to patients remaining in group psychotherapy, Int. J. Group Psychother. 7:264-275, 1957.
2. Johnson, J. A.: Group psychotherapy: A practical approach, New York, 1963, McGraw-Hill Book Co.
3. Slavson, S. R.: A textbook in analytic group psychotherapy, New York, 1964, International Universities Press.
4. Slavson, S. R.: Criteria for selection and rejection of patients for various kinds of group therapy, Int. J. Group Psychother. 5:3-30, 1955.
5. Corsini, R., and Lundin, W.: Group psychotherapy in the mid-west, Group Psychother. 8:316-320, 1955.
6. Rosenbaum, M., and Hartley, E.: A summary review of current practices of ninety-two group therapists, Int. J. Group Psychother. 12:194-198, 1962.
7. Bach, G.: Intensive group therapy, New York, 1954, Ronald Press.
8. Yalom, I. D.: The theory and practice of group psychotherapy, New York, 1975, Basic Books, Inc., pp. 236-237.
9. Cartwright, D., and Zander, A.: Group dynamics, New York, 1968, Harper & Row, Publishers.
10. Schutz, W.: The interpersonal underworld, Palo Alto, Calif., 1966, Science and Behavior Books.

11. Borgatta, E. F., and Bales, R. F.: Interaction of individuals in reconstituted groups, Sociometry **16**:302-320, 1953.
12. Borgatta, E. F., and Bales, R. F.: Task and accumulation of experience as factors in the interaction of small groups, Sociometry **16**:239-252, 1953.
13. Cattell, R. B., Saunders, D. R., and Stice, G. F.: The dimensions of syntality in small groups, J. Soc. Psychol. **28**:57-78, 1948.
14. Stone, A., Parloff, M., and Frank, J.: The use of diagnostic groups in a group therapy program, Int. J. Group Psychother. **4**:274-284, 1954.

5 □ The health care contract

A health care contract is an openly negotiated, clearly stated set of mutual expectations that indicates what the nurse and client can expect of each other regarding the client's health care. The contract consists of a set of shared objectives as well as a clear understanding of the structure and · process of arriving at mutually determined outcomes. The nurse must be specific about such issues as time and physical arrangements, fees, the type of treatment intervention that can be expected from the nurse, the involvement of other clients, and what is expected from the nurse, the other clients, and the client himself. When the nurse and client have arrived at a common understanding of what they can expect from each other, they have formulated a health care contract.

This health care contract is a reference point against which the nurse and the client can reflect any changes in their commitment to working together. It also serves as a useful measure of goal-directed progress in the client's health care situation. The contract can be renegotiated or terminated at any time. While it is in effect, it assists both the nurse and the client in being clear about the health care work they are doing together. Several specific aspects of the contract for group health care deserve elaboration.

PHYSICAL ARRANGEMENTS

One of the leadership functions of the group therapist is provision for the physical and temporal details of the group. The time, place, size, and physical arrangements for the group should all be clarified before the first group session and should be part of the initial contract between the leader and the group members. As with other group variables, there is no right or wrong way to determine the physical and temporal arrangements for the group. These arrangements should be made with the objectives, goals, and group members in mind. Group leaders must be cognizant of the relative advantages and disadvantages of their executive function decisions.

Time

Time arrangements for the group should be made with the schedules of the target population in mind. More than one eager group leader has been dismayed to realize that a number of group clients have other clinic or therapy appointments that conflict with the group meeting time. When dealing with clients in a multiple service hospital or agency, the time of day and day of the week during which the group is scheduled can become a complex juggling act.

The support and commitment of the agency for the health care group can greatly influence scheduling problems. Somehow an agency that is not really committed to the group can always find other activities or appointments for the clients during the group meeting time. Where the group is more highly regarded as an important aspect of the client's health care, other activities seem more easily scheduled around the group meeting time. This difference is an organizational fact of life and should provide ample motivation for the nurse to carefully secure organizational sanction before initiating a health care group.

If the target population for the group is ambulatory clients, the nurse will need to give careful consideration to the work, family, or class schedules of potential clients. A weight watchers group for working women might be scheduled during the lunch hour and near the work environment. A psychotherapy group whose members are professional people might best be scheduled on a weekday evening. An activity group for adolescents will need to meet after school hours or on a weekend when outings and more complex activities such as hikes and canoe trips can be more conveniently scheduled.

The length of time and frequency of meetings depends on the number of group members and the means by which the group will accomplish its objectives. The traditional psychotherapy group standard is to meet from 60 to 90 minutes once or twice a week. Some less traditional group therapists have experimented with less frequent group sessions that last for longer periods, e.g., once a week for 5 hours or once a month for a weekend marathon. If the therapeutic technique is one that requires that members practice certain newly learned behaviors in their work or social environments, more time between group sessions is desirable, e.g., meeting only once a week. If, on the other hand, the group is designed to teach clients how to live with diabetes and they are only in the hospital for 7 to 10 days for diagnosis and control of their diabetes, more frequent sessions over a 5- to 7-day period are most beneficial. Some group leaders choose to meet more frequently at first when the group members are in crisis or in need of more structure and later decrease to a once a week schedule.

If the group can accomplish its objectives through planning and partici- pating in activities, large blocks of time must be scheduled for cooking a dinner, visiting the local library, or planting and tending a garden. If an insight-oriented group has 10 members who need personal attention at each meeting, a 2½- or 3-hour session is required. Some aftercare groups meet for 30 to 40 minutes while 10 to 20 clients are waiting for their medications.

There is no magic formula for making decisions about time. The nurse must consider the needs of the group members, the size of the group, and the techniques by which the group objectives will be met in making time arrangements for the group.

Size

The size of the group should also be based on the needs of the clients and the techniques by which the group objectives will be met. Five or six members is usually considered to be the smallest group that will allow for diversity of membership and the development of the group interactional process. A group with more than ten to twelve members will usually break into smaller subgroups because of the difficulty in attending to a larger number of people all at once. If the group task lends itself to subgroupings, provision can be made for structuring a larger group. Most insight, or talk- oriented groups seem to function best with six to ten members. This is also a good size for learning–behavior change groups in which the members need time and assistance to practice new skills.

If there is a larger number of clients in need of a health care group than can be accommodated in a single group, several groups should be made available. A group that is too large to meet the needs of the individual members and the needs of the group as a whole is antitherapeutic. It is not good clinical practice to remain with too large a group simply because there are not enough funds available to start a second group. Client needs and the group task should be the primary consideration in determining group size.

Space and environment

Physical arrangements for the group should be made with the size and activities of the group clearly in mind. Generally speaking, clinicians should know much more about the effects of space and environment on people's physical and emotional health. Both the functional and esthetic aspects of the physical environment can have a measurable impact on the delivery and receiving of health care. What so often happens in overcrowded, under-budgeted health care agencies is that groups end up meeting in space that was designed for some other purpose. (If nurses are fortunate enough to be involved in the design and planning of a new health care facility, their first move should be to consult an architect or environmental psychologist regarding the space that will be designed for group interventions.)

Assuming that few nurses who initiate health care groups are in a position to design their own facilities, creative attention needs to be given to the selection of available existing space and the effect that the physical environment can have on group functioning. For example, people are less likely to make noise or speak loudly in a room that echoes. A conference room with a long table can interfere with openness and expression of feelings. A small room without ventilation will certainly constrain an exercise group. A group whose members are encouraged to share personal feelings in a confidential, safe atmosphere will never get under way unless the group meeting room is soundproof and free of interruptions. A playroom for young children should contain flooring and furniture on which the children can paint and play without concern for messing and an area where they can comfortably clean up after the group session. Marathon group sessions should be held where there are adequate sleeping, lavatory, and cooking facilities, as well as space for moving around physically.

I was once a co-leader of a treatment group for overtly psychotic inpatients. As luck would have it, the only room available for the group sessions was a large game room at the end of the ward. Previous groups of less disturbed patients had quit using this room because its size and high ceilings seemed to foster a feeling of interpersonal distance among group members and enhanced their resistances to sharing feelings together. The other therapist and myself were apprehensive about using the room but found that the clients were very comfortable there. The size of the room allowed the members to arrange themselves at a physical distance from each other at which they felt safe. Occasionally a group member would become agitated during the session and want to leave the group. We quickly learned to encourage such a member to move to another part of the room and to return to the group when comfortable. This was one way to meet the person's need for physical and emotional distance without totally removing him from the group. Both we and the group were more comfortable with this arrangement. When someone actually did need to leave the group (a rare occurrence), the ward and nursing staff were immediately available and there was minimal disruption to the group in returning the individual to the ward. Obviously, we had "located" an excellent meeting room for this particular group.

The point to be made is that the physical environment should facilitate rather than constrain group functioning. The furniture, heat, light, space, sound, and geographic location of the room will affect the group process. The nurse should be constantly aware of the effects of physical arrangements on the group and should plan the environment as much as possible to facilitate group functioning.

REIMBURSEMENT

Fee for service is an increasingly important issue for the profession of nursing. The ability to charge for direct services and to receive reimbursement from third-party carriers such as Blue Cross–Blue Shield and Medicaid affects both the financial independence and the professional respectability of health care services delivered by nurses. Since 1970 the American Nurses Association and numerous nursing practitioners have made slow but steady progress in obtaining health care legislation that recognizes the health care of professional nurses. It is important to keep the political, financial, and organizational aspects of fees for service for nurses in mind when examining the meaning of fees for health care groups.

The negotiation of a fee is an important aspect of arriving at a clear treatment contract. Most clients expect to pay for professional services they receive. Clients are more likely to be sure about whether or not they want a health care service if they are paying for it. The fee may be based on the client's ability to pay and may even consist of goods or services other than money. It has been my experience that clients who are committed to participating in a group as a way of changing or taking care of themselves have always been able to negotiate a reasonable fee or exchange of services. In one aftercare clinic, some clients are charged as little as 25 cents for each group session and most are proud that they can pay something for the service. For those who have more time than money, the staff has a list of odd jobs around the clinic that can substitute for payment. Many clinicians also believe that a fee is a useful influence in motivating clients to make use of their group experience.

When health professionals—and especially nurses—experience difficulty in determining and charging fees for their services, the problem is usually one centering around professional self-concept. Nurses are not socialized or educated to think of their services in terms of a professional fee. Most nurses are salaried employees, and their reimbursement is handled through an agency rather than directly with the client. They see themselves primarily as taking care of clients. But avoiding the issue of reimbursement does not help the client, the nurse, or the nursing profession. If a nurse is initiating a health care group within an agency, it is important that the cost of the group be determined with the administrator. If the nurse is a salaried employee, the time spent with the group each week can be easily figured as a percentage of the weekly salary. The agency may then decide how it will bill the clients or insurance carriers for this service. The nurse can then make these financial arrangements known to the group members. The group leader must make an exact statement of the fee or remuneration that will be expected of the client as part of the initial treatment contract. As a general rule, the process of charging for and paying for health care services increases the commitment of the agency, the nurse therapist, and the client to make optimum use of the services available.

PREPARATION OF CLIENTS

It is important to prepare clients for their health care group experience. The primary purpose of this preparation is the development of a set of mutual expectations between the client and the group leader. The client should emerge from this preparation with a clear and accurate picture of the objectives, structure, process, and outcomes of the health care group. Both client and nurse should have had the opportunity to share their expectations and arrive at a beginning contract, or agreement, regarding how they will work together within the group.

Self-referred clients or those sent to a health care group by another professional usually have some idea of why they need help and what will occur in the group. Depending on their prior preparation or previous treatment experiences, they will have a more or less accurate perception of what the group is all about. Some clients have been in groups before or know someone who participated in a health care group. These people will have some basis for comparison as the nurse describes the details of a particular group. Other clients will need to be taught about the process of delivering health care in groups.

If a number of clients have been identified who will possibly benefit from a specific type of health care group, the nurse can determine if each potential client shares the perception of his need. When the nurse and client agree on the need, they can begin discussing the ways in which the group will meet it. In voluntary groups the client is always in a position of accepting or rejecting the group as a desirable health care experience. This free choice should be made clear to potential clients in obtaining their commitment to work in the group.

There is no standard format for preparing clients for health care groups. In fact the process of preparing clients for a group experience is not even common practice among health professionals. A 1966 study by Yalom et al[1] indicated that clients who had been systematically prepared for their group therapy experience exhibited more faith in therapy and engaged in significantly more group and interpersonal interaction than the nonprepared clients as measured in the second and twelfth sessions. Because this was a research study, these clients were given a standard, predetermined type of preparation for group therapy. One might speculate that if their orientation had been more flexible and individualized, the results might have been even more dramatic.

I am convinced that a preparatory session prior to entering the group is a useful vehicle for developing a set of mutual expectations between the client and the group leader as well as facilitating the client's entry into the group. It is during this preparatory session that the most substantial groundwork is laid for a solid treatment contract. The following general format is suggested for preparing clients for health care groups.

Objectives

The client and nurse should each have an opportunity to share their reasons for being involved in the group. Since many people approach the health care system expecting to be told what to do, potential clients may be surprised when asked why they came and what they expect to get out of their group or health care experience. The nurse may need to help clients be specific and clear about what they want. I often ask potential clients, "If you get what you want out of the group, how will you be different 6 months from now?" When the reply is "I'll feel better" or "I'll be happier," the client should be asked specifically, with a behavioral picture, what that means for him personally. What will he be doing, where, with whom, and how will he be feeling about it? How is that different from what he is now doing? In that manner the nurse can begin to determine if the client has realistic expectations of himself and the group and if there is an agreement between his problem, his goals, and the objectives for the group. In some instances clients can be best served by referral to a more appropriate health care service. More often they can be helped to formulate more clear and realistic goals for themselves if I share my goals and objectives for the group. In effect the nurse is saying, "Here's what I can help you to accomplish." This is really the first and most important issue around which to establish mutual expectations.

Structure

It is useful, without going into too much detail, to share information with clients about the structure of the group. Many clients will express interest in the types of people who are in the group. I generally give a brief, general description of the group members and the problems on which they are working as a way of illustrating the group composition. Since there will be a fair amount of sharing in the group, it seems natural that clients will be interested in learning about their fellow group members.

The physical arrangements for the group are important to describe. Clients need to know the time, place, size, and setting of the group sessions. Often the time and location will influence whether or not an interested client can attend the group. I share with clients my own expectations for attendance and being notified in advance about any absence. I also have certain protective limits for my own groups that are made clear during the preparatory session. I expect that what occurs during the sessions will be treated as confidential information; that there will be no smoking or use of drugs or alcohol during group sessions; that clients will not physically hurt themselves or other group members; and that members will give at least 2 weeks notice before terminating therapy. Different therapists may require other protective limits of their group members. If there are certain rules or limits for the group, it is important that these be made clear as part of the treatment contract. Some therapists even develop a written list of expectations for their clients to sign before entering the group. This is a more concrete manifestation of the client's willingness to adhere to the limits and structure of the group.

The preparatory session is also an important time for any negotiations regarding the fee and method of payment for the group. As has been stated earlier, fees for health care services are important and should be handled as much as possible like business arrangements with therapeutic implications.

At this point, I usually stop and inquire regarding the client's reactions to the group structure that has been outlined. Does it seem safe and reasonable? Does it differ from what he expected and if so, how? Is he willing to accept this structure for the group? Invariably some of these issues will need to be renegotiated during the course of the group. It is important, however, that they be clearly stated and agreed on as part of the initial treatment contract.

Process

Part of the client's preparation for group involves a beginning introduction to what the group is all about. Just as health professionals have many questions regarding the benefits of group interventions, clients also often wonder how they will be helped in a health care group. If nurses are interested in utilizing the group process as a treatment vehicle, they will need to gradually educate their group members regarding what to expect. What will be the role of the leader? What will be expected of the client and what can be expected of other group members? I usually supply potential clients with a brief vignette of a typical group session as a way of explaining what the group is all about. This often answers a number of initial questions. If it seems that the client is still skeptical about the benefits of a group, it can be suggested that he ask other group members about their experiences when they began attending.

If there are certain predictable feelings that most group members experience, it is often useful to share these with new clients before they enter the group. The initial embarrassment of admitting that one needs help, the fear of being honest and open with a group of strangers, the concerns about not succeeding or changing in group, the conflict between taking care of other group members and getting one's own needs met, the feeling of wanting more of the therapist's time and attention, the feeling of closeness from sharing human experiences and problems with others, and the desire to have other members like you are all examples of personal feelings within the group. There seems to be some solace in knowing that one is not alone with certain experiences—that they are shared by others. Since the group is a new experience for most clients, it is helpful to be able to predict ahead of time what some of their feelings might be.

Some group leaders make use of this preparatory session to obtain a more detailed history of the client's problem and other relevant health care information. The need for background information will vary depending on the type of group and the treatment objectives. This information might be used by the nurse during the preparatory session to give the client a more specific description of how he might work on his problem in the group.

Outcomes

The final step of a good preparatory session is a restatement of the anticipated outcomes from participation in the health care group. By the end of the session, both client and nurse should be able to clearly state what they expect of each other within the context of the group and how they will evaluate success. The nurse will have a beginning relationship with the client that can then be transferred to the group setting. The nurse will also have a clear plan for how to work with the client within the group.

THE HEALTH CARE CONTRACT

By the time the client and nurse have completed their preparation session(s), they should have arrived at an initial health care contract. The words "initial health care contract" are used because contracting for health care or treatment is regarded as a dynamic process rather than a solid, stable state.

A health care contract as stated previously is an openly negotiated, clearly stated set of mutual expectations that indicates what the nurse and client can expect of each other regarding the client's health care. A good health care contract is open to renegotiation, alteration, or further clarification at any time as the client and nurse each change. Despite the possibility of altering the contract, both client and nurse should be able to clearly state their health care contract at any time. As Fig. 1 (p. 45) implies, a health care contract is influenced by the objectives and goals of the health care group. Furthermore, the health care contract influences and is influenced by the selection of clients, physical arrangements, fees, and the objectives, structure, process, and outcomes of the group that are discussed during the preparation of clients for the groups.

The initial contract is often a general "umbrella" agreement in which the client in effect says, "I want to alter my current health situation in this way, and I would like your help." The nurse responds, "I can help you do that, and here is how I propose to go about it. Here is what you can expect from me, and here is what I expect from you. Are you willing to participate?" As has been indicated, in a health care group the client's statement, "I want to alter my current health situation," and the nurse's statement, "I can help you do that," become the shared objectives part of the contract. The nurse's statement, "Here is how I propose to go about it," includes an explanation of the process of the health care group, the other clients who will be in the group, the physical arrangements, the fees, and a statement of the anticipated outcomes. When both nurse and client agree to proceed with the health care group, they have formulated an important initial health care contract.

As the client, the nurse, and the group actually become involved in the process of working toward the group objectives, the health care contract is likely to become much more specific and may be gradually altered. The increasing specificity comes from the work that each client does in meeting his health care objective. For example, a client's initial contract may be to lose 100 pounds. In the beginning sessions that client may agree to collect specific information about his eating behavior. Later, focus of the contract may shift to manageable behavioral and/or attitudinal changes that will decrease eating and produce weight loss. In the process of working on this problem, the nurse and client may decide that it is essential that the client learn how to relate to other people without food being involved. The immediate contract may then shift to working on developing more direct, close relationships, but with the primary overall objective still being that of losing weight.

From session to session and week to week, the health care contract should be clear. When it appears that what the nurse and the client or group are working on is becoming vague, it is time to raise the question, "What is our contract?" This will help the nurse and group to once again focus their work and reestablish their mutual expectations.

In summary, we have explored the ways in which the objectives and goals of the group influence the group structure. When the nurse is structuring a health care group, the selection of clients, physical arrangements of the group, fees, and preparation of clients are all central considerations. What should emerge from this development of group objectives and structure is an initial health care contract between the nurse and the group and among group members. Once all of these pieces are in place, the nurse and the group are ready to confront the much more exciting, but less specific and predictable, issues of group process.

REFERENCE

1. Yalom, I. D., Houts, P. S., Newell, G., and Rand, K. H.: Preparation of patients for group therapy, Arch. Gen. Psychiatry **17:**416-427, 1967.

Section III

Intervention — small group process

Group process is a general concept that refers to just about everything that happens within the group during the life of the group. It includes not only the content of what is said or done in the group, but how members interact with each other, the timing of those interactions, and the roles that the leader and members play in relation to one another. Some group leaders and members refer to the group as if it had a being or life of its own that was something more than merely the sum of all the individual members and their interactions. At times they will refer to "the group's level of anxiety" or ask, "How does the group feel about that?"

In fact every group does develop a process that is unique unto itself. The specifics of this process are impossible to predict ahead of time even if the leader knows all of the members individually before the group begins. There are, however, some general group process issues with which all groups must deal in one way or another. The issues of the role and style of the leader, the roles that specific members will play in the group, the patterns of communication and types of power and influence that will be exerted within the group are common group process issues. The degree of clarity and agreement regarding group norms and goals are issues confronted by all groups. This section examines these group process issues, their development in various types of health care groups, and possible interventions the nurse might consider as group leader.

It is difficult to learn to observe group process. The role of the group leader is similar to a traffic control analyst flying over an expressway in a helicopter at rush hour. At any given moment, the traffic analyst can bring the helicopter down close enough to observe the people in a single car, fly high enough to analyze the flow of traffic at one large interchange, or fly even higher to observe the entire freeway system. No matter which level the traffic control analyst chooses, something will probably be missed that might have been observed by flying at a different level. The flying level depends on the major objective for the day. If the traffic control analyst wishes to count the number of single-passenger vehicles, the flying level will be quite low to pick up this specific information. If the objective is to analyze the volume of traffic that flows into an interchange from each of four major expressway arteries, the flying level will be a bit higher. At various times during peak traffic periods, the analyst's major goal may be to spot accidents,

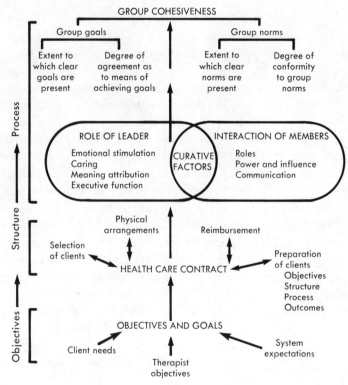

Fig. 2
Model of small group variables—objectives, structure, and process (adapted from a model by M. Loomis and J. Dodenhoff, 1970).

call for emergency help, and give directions for re-routing traffic. In this situation, the analyst might fly quite high until a slow down or stop in the normal flow of traffic is observed and then zero in directly to the source of the problem.

The group leader acts in a way similar to that of the traffic control analyst. At times the leader may be attending primarily to what is going on with one individual member, then to how the other group members are responding to that member, and then to how the specific situation fits into the process of what has been occurring in the group. The skilled group leader is able to attend to all of these levels of activity at one time and decide where and how to intervene. Whether the leader is attending to it or not, there is always a group process level of activity. This section is intended to assist the beginning group leader to identify these group process issues and plan health care group interventions with the process of the group in mind. Attention will also be given to when and how the group leader might choose to focus on the overall group process and when to address specific individual concerns of members. The end result should be that the nurse is able to use the group process to the therapeutic benefit of the clients.

Fig. 2 is used as an outline for presenting the ideas in this section. The model demonstrates the impact of group objectives and group structure on the process of the group. Each of the components of group process (interaction of members, role of the therapist, curative factors, and group cohesiveness) will be discussed as they relate to the phases of various types of health care groups.

6 □ Initial group concerns

Most people are concerned about entering a new situation. The uncertainty of the situation usually causes some anticipatory thoughts and oftentimes anxiety about what will occur. Will the other people like me? What will be expected of me? Will I get something out of it? What is going to happen? These and other similar questions about the unknown can produce much anxiety.

When group members have had some preparation for a health care group experience, they have received information that will answer a few of their factual questions. This information may not, however, allay their own interpersonal concerns. "Will the group help me?" is a question that can only be answered with certainty after the fact—when the actual helping has occurred. In the meantime, and especially before the group has developed a clear pattern of working together, members will make up their own answers to this and similar questions. Unfortunately, people who are uncertain about their own interpersonal capabilities and whether or not they can be helped will often assume the worst: "Perhaps no one will like me" or "Maybe I can't be helped."

Assuming that many people will enter a group experience with these concerns, they will approach the group in a cautious manner. Group members can be expected to check out each other and the therapist to determine if the group is safe. Yalom[1] has described this period of initial testing as the "In or Out" period in the group's life. All of the members will be determining whether or not the group is a safe place to let down their social facade and share their problems, concerns, and questions.

74

INTERACTION OF MEMBERS

The first attempt on the part of group members to handle their initial concerns about the group will often center around the development of roles. There are two primary definitions of the term "role," either one of which may be considered appropriate at various times in small groups. The first refers to the part or character that an actor presents in a play. The second refers to a proper or customary function as in "the role of the therapist."

In their initial discomfort, group members will often search out or develop a role that is familiar to them from previous group or individual experiences. One member who is frightened may attempt to structure the group by proposing an agenda, suggesting that the members introduce themselves, and in general appearing to be in control of the situation. Another frightened member may withdraw into a silent corner alternately hoping and fearing that no one will notice him. Yet another member will handle her anxiety by being concerned and supportive of other group members.

Two factors should be kept in mind regarding the initial development of roles in a group. The first is that the search for a comfortable, predictable role in the group is related to the initial discomfort and uncertainty experienced by members during the process of entering a new group. The second is that the roles members attempt to assume in a group are very similar, if not identical, to the roles they play in other groups and relationships.

Take, for example, Ralph, who entered the first meeting of an outpatient psychotherapy group by arriving 15 minutes late, spilling his coke on the carpet, and interrupting several members while they were talking. The therapist was not surprised to learn after several sessions that Ralph was in serious danger of losing his job and was becoming increasingly depressed by the negative feedback he was receiving from his roommates. The role of "clod" that he had assumed in the group was typical of the way in which he set up other relationships outside the group.

Closely related to the development of roles is the development of patterns of power and influence, another phenomenon that occurs during the initial phase of most small groups. Yalom[1] has characterized the resolution of power and influence issues as the "Top or Bottom" phase in the group's life. While there is no predetermined time period a group must spend resolving the issues of power and influence, a group in which these issues are not clarified will experience difficulty in accomplishing its primary objective. Most health care groups have a designated leader who is usually a health professional. Lay groups will often elect or select a chairperson for a specific period.

Regardless of how the group addresses the issues, it must find answers to the questions, "Who is in charge?" and "Who will be influential in the group?" French and Raven[2] have identified five bases of social power that may also be applicable to health care groups: reward, coercive, legitimate, referent, and expert powers. Reward and coercive powers both refer to the recipients' perception of the influencing agent as being capable of rewarding or punishing them for their responses to the attempt at influence. Legitimate power stems from internalized values in the recipient and dictates that the influence has a legitimate right to influence him and that he is obligated to accept this influence. Referent power is based on the attraction that the recipient feels for the person attempting to influence him—on his desire to be like, to identify with, and to be closely associated with that person. Expert power refers to the recipient's perception that the individual attempting to influence is better informed than he is himself on the topic under discussion.

That all sounds very straightforward until one realizes that what occurs in most groups is a mixture of bases of power and influence. The nurse may be the legitimate leader of a support group for high-risk pregnant women. Since the group is a voluntary, outpatient experience, the nurse has no clear base of reward or coercive power. The hospital is not likely to refuse to deliver the baby if a member does not attend group sessions, nor should this be a part of the contract. The nurse may be an expert in group process, but she may never have had a baby, or at least not under high-risk conditions. She must therefore share her expert base of power and influence with other group members who can speak from their own feelings and experiences. Referent power may also be shared by the leader and/or several group members depending on their interpersonal attractiveness to the group.

All groups have task-related needs and social maintenance needs that must be met. The mix between these two types of need may vary from group to group or from time to time within a group. Even a committee that is very clearly task oriented will need to attend to its social maintenance needs by scheduling an occasional coffee break. A social group will need to attend to periodic business such as deciding on the date for a picnic. While the primary objective of health care groups is therapeutic, they also have task-related and social maintenance needs that must be met. The degree and type of power and influence exercised by the leader and group members will to a large degree be related to each person's facility for helping the group to meet both its objectives and needs.

In most health care groups the bases of power and influence are shared because the interaction of members is therapeutically beneficial. In some groups one of the members may attempt to establish herself as the self-proclaimed expert and leader of the group. In other groups the members may attempt to idealize the leader as the only legitimate expert on the topic. The nurse needs to recognize both of these extremes as being detrimental to the group process. When they occur early in the life of the group, they can be dealt with as symptomatic of the members' initial concerns about the operation of the group. The nurse may need to remind the members of their initial contract regarding the sharing of influence and information among all members and the leader. It is important that the leader recognize the unique contributions of each member and model this sharing of power and influence.

The third and final issue around which group members demonstrate their initial concerns is developing patterns of communication. On the surface this appears to be a matter of resolving who will talk to whom about what. Yalom[1] characterizes the underlying issue as "Near or Far." The resolution of the prior concerns regarding roles, power, and influence now leaves the group free to deal with just how open and/or closed the members will be with each other. While roles, power and influence, and communication are certainly all interrelated issues, communication is the most crucial in health care groups.

A number of communication variables can actually be quantified. The group leader could have someone record the number of times member X talks to member Y, the length of time per interaction, and the content of their exchanges. The leader could also quantify the frequency of initiated and received interactions for each member and emerge with a very specific picture of what has occured in the group—who talks with whom, how much, and about what. While this sociometric approach to analyzing group interactions is perhaps one of the more accurate, it is also one of the more time-consuming methods if done routinely, carefully, and thoroughly analyzed.

Analyzing the patterns of communication within a group is a difficult task, whether done empirically or impressionistically. For the beginning group leader, there seem to be literally hundreds of things that need attention. Who tends to raise questions? Who gives answers? Who responds to the emotional content in what is being said? Who does not say anything? How much are members interacting with each other? Who is asking for special attention from the leader? Who changes the topic when feelings are being expressed? How is humor utilized in the group? The list is probably endless and there are no two, five, or ten questions that are most important. What is important is to recognize patterns of communication as they emerge. To do this, the group leader needs to be hovering, like the traffic control analyst, at an intermediate height above the group. The leader needs to watch communication patterns as they emerge as well as attend to the specifics of what the group members are saying to each other and to the leader. It is sometimes useful to construct a general diagram of the pattern of communication following each group session. The following are some examples from the high-risk pregnancy group referred to earlier. (The ideas for these diagrams were generated by the work of Eric Berne.[3])

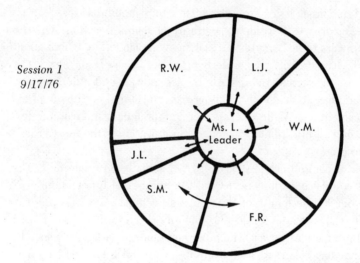

Session 1
9/17/76

In this session R. W. and W. M. dominated most of the group time (as indicated by the large area assigned to each) and kept Ms. L., the group leader, busy answering their questions and responding to their obvious anxiety. J. L. and L. J. handled their anxiety by remaining silent (smaller spaces) yet listening to everything that was said. S. M. and F. R. demonstrated a direct interest in sharing their common experiences—this is the second pregnancy for both—and the leader is interested in encouraging their interactions with each other and then with the other group members. The arrows to and from the leader indicate the relative frequency of interactions to and from each member.

Session 5
10/15/76

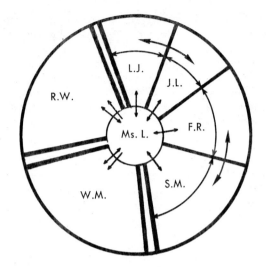

By the fifth session, L. J. and J. L. had quietly found each other and were using each other for support and information. F. R. and S. M. had continued to develop their relationship and were reaching out to L. J. and J. L. The leader's role with these four members was to supply necessary information and to encourage the sharing and support they were receiving from each other. R. W. and W. M. had effectively walled themselves off from each other and the other group members (double lines). The leader had begun to directly point out the manner in which they are maintaining their "differentness" and not receiving help from the other group members.

Session 12
12/3/76

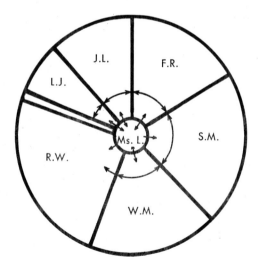

The leader is now maintaining fairly equal contact with all group members and is able to back off periodically and deal with more general group process issues. L. J. and J. L. are still the quietest members but are clearly involved in a meaningful way with the group. There is still an interaction barrier between R. W. and the quieter group members, however she is gradually beginning to enter into the process of the group. As she is getting her own needs met and becoming less anxious, she is better able to relate and is doing so through being more direct with the more assertive members—especially W. M.

The above is an illustration of the importance of ongoing attention to the patterns of communication among group members. It demonstrates the type of group process observations that the leader can make during the initial group sessions. The roles and types of power and influence exerted by group members can often be observed to coincide with the pattern of communication.

In this example, R. W. established herself as the demanding helpless child beginning with the first session. W. M. assumed the role of the jealous younger sister whose only hope for attention was to compete with R. W. for the therapist. L. J. and J. L. became the quiet, compliant observers who denied their own needs in order not to rock the boat. F. R. and S. M. were the practical cousins who remained apart from competition yet figured out a way to get their needs met by each other. For each of these women, the roles they assumed in the group were familiar to them. Eventually the nurse managed to exert legitimate and expert bases of power to alter the roles and patterns of communication originally established by the group members.

ROLE OF THE LEADER

The role of the leader is an important factor to consider at each phase in the life of the group. At first glance it would appear that deciding what the leader should do in any given situation is far too complex to even write about. Indeed, there are a multitude of factors that an experienced group leader quickly takes into consideration before intervening. The factors of personal style and experience are very important, and at times it appears that the experienced leader just intuitively knows what to do.

It is important, however, to attempt to bring some order to the apparent confusion behind the questions of a beginning group leader. "But how did you know to do that?" "What should I have done?" "I didn't know what to do, so I didn't do anything." Until a personal style and experience base in leading groups is developed, the nurse will probably rely more heavily on a theoretical understanding of group process. The functions of the therapist, the objectives of the group, and the phase of group development will be discussed from the perspective of the influence they have on the role of the group leader.

There are very few right or wrong answers to the question, "What should I have done?" Five experienced group leaders might very well offer five different solutions to the same situation. And each solution might be effective given the appropriate mix of leader, group members, and phase in the group's development. The science of working with groups is such that it is much easier to theorize after the fact about the relative merits of a leader's intervention than it is to predict or prescribe its effectiveness. Any nurse who is inexperienced in working with groups should arrange for supervision from a more experienced group leader. This supervision can be utilized to both understand what has gone on in past group sessions and to predict what might be expected in future sessions. The nurse should receive guidance in analyzing and planning interventions.

Apart from the moral, ethical, and legal considerations involved in delivering any kind of health care, there is very little that is right or wrong in groups. There are primarily relative advantages and disadvantages. It is not right or wrong to allow smoking during a group session. The leader merely needs to consider what might happen if smoking is either allowed or forbidden. When smoking is forbidden by the leader, the issue has been effectively removed from the group decision-making process. The leader loses the opportunity to observe how the group will handle the issue when it arises, because the rule has already been made. If the objectives of the group do not include work on decision making and conflict resolution, little has been lost. In fact, the group may progress more smoothly toward its goal because the leader has firmly handled one potential source of conflict. In a group where the authority of the leader is being challenged, the smoking issue may resurface later in the form of a challenge by one or several group members. The leader may then choose to focus the group on the major issue of control that is underlying the questions about not smoking.

As can be seen from this example, the leader's behavior definitely affects the group process. In any group or any group situation, the leader must consider the relative trade-offs involved with the effects of any actions. Most leader interventions are neigher right nor wrong—merely effective or ineffective, depending on the group.

In a 1973 study by Lieberman et al,[4] four basic leadership functions were determined to account for almost 75% of the activities of the seventeen group leaders in the study. The researchers identified these leadership functions as: emotional stimulation, caring, meaning-attribution, and executive function.

Emotional stimulation was described as the leader's behaviors that encouraged the group members to actively share their feelings. The leader's role was to confront, challenge, exhort, and model the revelation of personal values and feelings. This meant that the leader was very actively involved and participating with the group. In fact, the leaders who were rated highest on emotional stimulation ran very leader-centered groups. Their use of referent power meant that much of the member activity focused on the leader as either a positive or negative reaction to the leader's personalized style. The primary objective of emotional stimulation is to generate feelings on which the group members can work.

Caring as a leadership function involved the modeling of warm, accepting, positive feelings to assist the group in developing an accepting and supportive climate in which the members could work on their problems. The focus of the caring was not so much on feeling positively about the leader as on the acceptance and caring for each other by the group members.

Meaning-attribution was the leadership function by which the group leaders developed understanding of feelings and behaviors within the group. This function calls on the expert power of the leader to help the group members understand *why* certain feelings and behaviors were occurring. Meaning-attribution recognizes the importance of the cognitive or intellectual element in changing behavior. For many people it is not enough to have had a certain experience—they want to understand it.

Executive function included all of the organizing, limit-setting, and management activities of the group leader. Starting and stopping the group on time, asking members to speak, and setting rules for member behavior are all examples of the executive function of the leader. Leaders who rated high on executive function acted more as facilitators or traffic engineers than as involved members of the group. In many ways the executive function can be described as the exact opposite of the emotional stimulation function.

One of the many interacting findings of the Lieberman et al study involved the relationship of these four basic group leadership functions. The leaders rated as most effective in the study were those who were moderate in their degree of emotional stimulation, high in caring, high in meaning-attribution, and moderate in executive function. What emerges from the data in this study is the following general profile of the effective group leader:

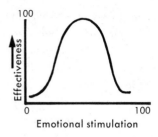

Emotional stimulation

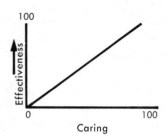

Caring

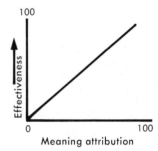

Meaning attribution

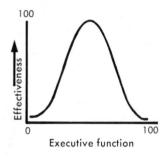

Executive function

The reader is reminded that this study was conducted on encounter and therapy-type groups with university students as the group members. It is not yet clear how these groups are similar to or different from different types of health care groups. There is a need for clinical validation and nursing research on health care groups similar to that conducted by Lieberman et al. In the meantime, the four leadership functions outlined above provide a useful point of reference for discussing the role of the leader in health care groups.

The role of the leader during the initial phase of the group is to a large degree influenced by the type of group and the initial concerns the group is confronting. Generally speaking, a support group will be placing much emphasis on the caring function of the group leader, while a task group requires a higher degree of executive function. A socialization group may need equally high amounts of caring and executive functioning, while a learning–behavior change group requires a leader who places more emphasis on meaning-attribution and executive functioning. Human relations training groups tend to have leaders who place much emphasis on emotional stimulation and meaning-attribution, while successful psychotherapy groups will follow the pattern of moderate emotional stimulation, high caring, high meaning-attribution, and moderate executive function described by Lieberman et al.

Since it is not possible to prescribe the exact levels or proportions of each of these leadership functions for each type of health care group, there will of necessity be some trial and error involved. The nurse will need to experiment with the role of leader until the blend of leadership functions is found that is personally acceptable and that fits the needs and objectives of the group. The leadership functions of emotional stimulation, caring, meaning-attribution, and executive function provide a useful point of reference for examining one's role as group leader.

For example, in assisting a new health care group to deal with its initial concerns, the nurse should use a unique mixture of leadership functions. Because the group members are usually anxious and uncertain about their entry into a health care group, the nurse should approach the group with a high degree of caring and meaning-attribution as a way of both recognizing the needs of the group and providing information that will decrease their uncertainty. Since the new members are probably already anxious, the nurse should minimize the emotional stimulation function.

The executive function of the group leader can be varied initially, depending on the type of group and how much responsibility the group members can assume for their own functioning. It is clearly a function that involves some of the trade-offs mentioned earlier in this chapter. Most generally stated, the greater the degree of structure (executive functioning) provided by the leader, the less likelihood there is for group members to act out or search for the boundaries of what will be acceptable behavior in the group.

If the above relationships are true, the leader can determine just how much of the group's effort is to be directed toward developing the structure of the group. In a short-term group, it may be more practical for the leader to assume responsibility for providing the group structure so that the group can devote most of its energy to its stated task or learning objective. In groups of small children it may not be developmentally reasonable to expect the youngsters to define what will be considered acceptable behavior. On the other hand, the development of group norms and goals may be the primary learning objective for a group of adolescents or an aftercare group of recently discharged state hospital clients. It is important to realize that each group will differ, depending to some degree on how much structure is provided by the leader.

CURATIVE FACTORS

One final consideration in dealing with the initial concerns of a health care group is the importance of curative factors. Yalom[1] speculates that the curative factors that influence change within a group are different at the various stages of a group's life. As mentioned under the heading "Group process" in Chapter 3, the instillation of hope, universality, imparting of information, and altruism all appear to be significant curative factors in the early stage of group functioning. The leader should therefore be prepared to maximize these factors. For example, it is important that group members are provided an opportunity to get to know each other and share their similarities and differences during the first several sessions. They need to learn that they are not alone and isolated, that they begin to experience that others have changed, and that they too can be helped with their problems. Whether this opportunity is structured in the form of a group assignment or comes about from the natural process of the group, the leader must be aware of its importance. If this type of sharing does not occur, it can be brought to the attention of the group as having significance for their future work together.

The above discussion of initial group concerns is not exhaustive. An attempt has been made to highlight some of the major group member and leader concerns during the group's initial sessions. No doubt each clinician will be able to add new information to this discussion following their own initial experiences with health care groups.

REFERENCES

1. Yalom, I. D.: The theory and practice of group psychotherapy, New York, 1975, Basic Books.
2. French, J. R. P., Jr., and Raven, B.: The bases of social power. In Cartwright, D., and Zander, A. (eds.): Group dynamics, New York, 1968, Harper & Row, Publishers.
3. Berne, E.: Principles of group treatment, New York, 1966, Oxford University Press.
4. Lieberman, M. A., Yalom, I. D., and Miles, M. B.: Encounter groups: First facts, New York, 1972, Basic Books.

7 □ The development of group cohesiveness

Group cohesiveness has already been discussed as a curative factor and a mechanism by which people change in groups. Research evidence in the group dynamics[1] and group therapy[2] literature strongly indicates that the degree and nature of group cohesiveness greatly affects the process and outcomes of many different types of groups. Given the potential impact of this complex variable, the development of group cohesiveness is being emphasized here as an important phase in the life of health care groups. Special consideration will be given to the nature of group cohesiveness and role of the leader in fostering group cohesion. Potential threats to group cohesiveness will be explored along with the leader and group interventions that are effective in countering these threats.

Festinger has defined group cohesiveness as "the resultant of all forces acting on members to remain in the group."[3] For each individual group member this attraction to the group can be viewed in terms of (1) the needs of the person that can be met in the group, (2) the objectives and goals of the group that relate to his needs, (3) the person's expectation that the group will have beneficial consequences for him, and (4) the person's perception of the effectiveness of the group in providing valuable outcomes. In most instances group cohesiveness is described in terms of the positive pull or attraction that the group exerts on its members; however, in some settings there are also negative external pressures exerted on members that must be recognized.

Group cohesiveness is regarded by Yalom as the analogue of the relationship in individual therapy: "It is obvious that the group therapy analogue of the patient-therapist relationship is a broader concept, encompassing the patient's relationship to his group therapist, to the other group members, and to the group as a whole."[4] Cohesiveness is both a cause and an effect of the interaction process that occurs within groups. Several research studies[2,5-7] have demonstrated the positive correlation between high attraction to the group and positive outcomes in group therapy. Based on this evidence, the development of group cohesiveness in health care groups is discussed in this chapter as a potential determinant of positive member outcomes of the group experience.

Group cohesiveness is the glue that holds groups together, helps them over rough spots, allows them to fend off outside threats, and, in the case of health care groups, helps the members to change. Most people can recognize a cohesive group when they see one. The members usually feel good about one another and about their group identification. They are loyal to each other and to the goals and values of the group. They may even take on similar behavior, styles of dress, or mannerisms. When there is an issue to be resolved or a task to be done, they mobilize their collective forces, decide on a method of approaching the problem, and move readily toward resolution. The members of such a group seem to enjoy spending time together, look forward to their meetings, and may even plan extra times to be together. Anyone who has been a member of such a cohesive group usually recalls the experience with positive affect and may even wish to reconstruct such a group in the future.

It is not always clear to group members or leaders how to go about developing the type of cohesiveness described above. Some research[8-10] indicates that similarities among members will increase member attraction to the group. However, the reader is encouraged to think back to the discussion regarding selection of members in Chapter 4. Along which dimensions is homogeneity or heterogeneity of group members to be determined? In health care groups, as in most voluntary social or work groups, member similarity is most effectively defined in terms of the mutually agreed on objectives and goals of the group when the group is first beginning. Group goals are therefore the first building block of group cohesiveness in a health care group.

GROUP GOALS

The importance of clarifying the objectives and goals of the group with respect to the client needs, therapist objectives, and system expectation has already been emphasized. When the nurse is selecting members for a certain type of health care group, there is often a tendency to gloss over minor discrepancies regarding the goals of the group. Especially if the nurse is trying to gather just one or two more members so that the group can get started, there is a temptation to assume that once the client is in the group he will see how important it is to subscribe to the goals of the group. This is a particularly important problem in a new, small group where the sharing of common goals is so essential to the development of group cohesiveness.

A laboratory study by Raven and Rietsema[11] indicated that the incentive value of a particular group goal for a particular person will depend not only on its content but also on how explicitly the goal is formulated, how clear the paths for goal attainment are, and the likelihood of successful achievement of the goal. If these findings can be generalized to health care groups, it is no wonder then that many support groups whose objectives are to "help people talk about their problems," suffer from membership and attendance problems and, in many instances, early termination of the group.

The health care provider must be as specific as possible about the goals that are to be accomplished in the group. This specificity allows potential members to compare their own needs with the objectives and goals of the group and to make a definite commitment to pursuing the goals of the group as a member. It will not help the group if an individual member learns after he is in the group that the group goal of member weight loss is different from his personal objective of understanding why he over eats. Early terminations are disruptive to group process and interfere with the development of group cohesiveness. Therefore, goal compatibility should be determined early, hopefully during the selection and preparation of clients for health care groups.

The extent to which definite goals are present and the degree of agreement as to the means of achieving those goals will greatly influence the development of cohesiveness in health care groups. Both of these factors are obstensibly under the control of the health care provider. In voluntary groups, especially, the group leader and potential members can reach some agreement about the group goals and methods of achieving those goals before the group even starts or before the leader and potential member make a commitment to work together in the group.

A precise statement on the leader's part is essential. For example, "This is a weight-loss group in which the members contract to lose a certain amount of weight over a specified period. You and I will develop your personal behavior modification plan. The members work within the group to reinforce each other sticking to their plans and losing weight"; or "This is a transactional analysis group for people who want to change something about themselves—their feelings about themselves, how they relate to other people, or their current life situations. You decide what you want to work on, and the group and therapist will help you"; or, "We have found that parents who have a critically ill youngster often feel better if they have some-one with whom they can talk and with whom they can share common experi-ences. We hope this group will serve that purpose for you."

Very often the members will need to have the method of achieving the group goals clarified once they are in the group. Some of this clarification is a continuation of the educational process that was begun during their prepa-ration for the group. In a highly structured group, the means of achieving the group goals becomes very clear from the outset. In a less structured group, the leader and members will probably need to periodically review the ways in which the group and its members can accomplish their mutual goals. These methods, once established, practiced, and modified, become part of the norms of the group.

GROUP NORMS

Group norms refers to the standards for behavior that are normative or most usual within the group. Cartwright and Zander[12] describe "pressures to uniformity" that occur in most groups and serve the functions of (1) helping the group to accomplish its goals, (2) helping the group to maintain itself as a group, (3) helping the members to develop validity or reality for their opin-ions, and (4) helping members to define their relations to their social sur-roundings. Group norms become the spoken and unspoken rules for acceptable behavior within the group, and the group functioning is dis-rupted when members deviate from the norms.

In a health care group, norms can develop in a variety of ways. During the preparation of clients for group membership, the leader may very well describe what members are expected to do in the group. They may be told that the group is a place to talk about feelings, share common problems about raising children, work on changing some aspect of themselves, or dis-cuss relationships with parents and teachers. In this manner the leader begins to prompt the behavior that will occur in the group. The leader may also have certain rules or expectations of all group members such as regular attendance, no smoking during the sessions, or coming on time. These behaviors become part of the normative expectations for group membership.

Once the group begins meeting, the leader and members interact in the development of group norms. During the initial phase of the group's life, much of the tentative exploration of members revolves around their attempts to answer the question, "What is expected and acceptable behavior here?" Assuming that a health care group is probably different from other groups with which the members are familiar, this search for expectations and acceptance forms a substantial portion of the group's early work. If the group is a highly structured or task-oriented group, the leader will be more actively involved in clarifying the group norms. On the other hand, if the leader is less involved in determining the behavioral norms and gives the group this responsibility, the development of norms may continue throughout the entire life of the group.

As the group members develop their roles within the group, they will have an impact on the group norms and vice versa. Lieberman et al[2] found a high correlation between the members who were most influential in the groups in their study and the degree to which they engaged in behaviors consistent with the group norms (risk taking, spontaneity, openness, self-disclosure, expressivity, group facilitation, and support). These group leaders, or influencers, were also found to have significantly higher outcome ratings at the end of the group experience.

Members who are considered influential or assume a leadership role in the group are usually those who pursue the group goals themselves and facilitate the movement of other group members toward the group objectives. Their behavior is reinforced by the group leader and often modeled by the other members. At times the nurse is fortunate enough to have a member who has been in another health care group. This member can make a valuable contribution to the development and modeling of positive normative behavior in the group.

Enabling norms are those expected and accepted behaviors that move the group and its members toward their objectives. In a weight loss group enabling norms might include developing a plan for weight loss, reporting each week on one's progress, and members praising each other for their actual weight loss. In a psychotherapy group, enabling norms might include talking openly about one's problems, expressing feelings rather than intellectualizing, and providing support and caring when other members are hurting. What becomes clear from these examples is the interdependence between goals and norms. Enabling group norms are actually a vehicle for moving the group toward attainment of its goals.

Restrictive norms, on the other hand, are those expected and accepted behaviors that impede the group's progress toward its goals. At times a group may develop restrictive norms because of the members' anxieties about or disagreement with the leader's goals and expectations for the group. Examples of restrictive norms include such behaviors as laughing at members who are having difficulty, changing the subject when someone is expressing feelings, or not tolerating disagreement within the group. Generally speaking, restrictive norms within a health care group are unhealthy if allowed to continue without leader intervention.

ROLE OF THE LEADER

The role of the leader in the development of group cohesiveness relates very directly to the goals and norms of the group. In effect, the goals and norms are the vehicles the leader can use to develop and nurture group cohesiveness. Reference has already been made to the role of the leader in establishing the goals and beginning norms of the group during the process of structuring the group and selecting and preparing members. Because the leader is often the initial link between a new member and the group, the leader's statement of goals and norms is extremely influential. A major portion of the leader's responsibility for executive functioning centers around structuring the goals and norms of the group to maximize the group's health care potential.

Once the group is started, the leader may move gradually toward a posture of sharing executive functions with the group. Less of the leader's energy and time are devoted to the task of structuring the group, and more attention is given to assisting the group to develop norms that will facilitate attainment of the group goals and objectives. During the group's initial sessions, the leader may have readily responded to questions as a way of reducing member anxiety and uncertainty. Gradually, however, the leader should encourage group members to ask questions of each other and foster group discussion of relevant issues as a way of developing group cohesiveness. As the group engages in more mutual sharing of feelings and experiences, it is important that the leader comment positively and thereby reinforce increased member interaction. As the group members work collaboratively to develop shared norms and goals, the level of group cohesiveness will increase. Members will assist in the executive functions previously fulfilled by the leader, thus freeing the leader to focus more on the process that is developing within the group.

While group cohesiveness is developing, it is important that the leader increase the stimulation function by paying special attention to any reinforcement of interactions that support the goals and norms of the group. If the goal of the group is a specific change in member behavior, the leader should actively acknowledge members who have made positive changes. The leader should also encourage the group members to acknowledge each other's progress. Comments such as, "I'm pleased so many of you noticed Joan is less depressed tonight," or, "What do the rest of you think about Joan's recent changes?" are often very facilitative.

The stimulation and caring functions of the leader are equally important to the formation of group cohesiveness. As the leader stimulates the expression of feelings, the change of behavior, or other interpersonal risk taking on the part of the members, it is imperative that this be done from a caring position. People are not likely to make interpersonal changes or openly share themselves with others if they do not feel safe. The leader must offer not only permission to change, but also a protective environment in which new behaviors can be learned. For example, a young mother who shares her feelings of anger at becoming pregnant for the sixth time is less likely to be that open again with a group that chastises her for not loving her children. A caring group response would consist of acknowledging the validity of her feeling and how difficult it might have been to share it with others. Perhaps other group members have had similar feelings and can share their own feelings and how they dealt with the situation. The young mother can then be assisted to decide what she will do about her own situation in an atmosphere of acceptance and caring. One such event well-handled by the group and leader can have a marked affect on the goals, norms, and subsequent cohesiveness of the group.

The leader becomes a role model for the group in the development of group goals and norms. When the leader listens with interest, verbally reinforces, ignores, or actively disapproves of certain group interactions or member behaviors, the rest of the group incorporates what is being modeled. It is in this manner that the leader can clearly influence the formation of enabling rather than restrictive norms. For example, when the leader discourages the expression of negative feelings, the group will probably have difficulty dealing with anger or may even ignore that emotion entirely. But the leader's silent acceptance of member lateness and absences will assist the group in ignoring the importance of attendance to the group functioning.

The leader must make clear the interdependence of group members in accomplishing the group goals. In a study of group-contingent reinforcement by Loomis,[13] six chronic patients in a state hospital were offered rewards (money and outings) if the entire group performed certain target behaviors related to work and grooming. Even though this regressed group of men had no previous commitment to each other prior to this research project, they were readily able to comprehend their interdependence in achieving the group-contingent reinforcement. On their own initiative, the men found ways of helping each other with their cafeteria jobs, assisted each other in obtaining clothing on the designated days, and even assisted one more regressed member in learning to shave himself.

The member's caring about each other generalized to behaviors other than those targeted for reinforcement. One day after the men had received their pay for working and achieving the target behaviors for the study, one group member offered to keep John's money for him so that he would not give it away to other patients who regularly approached him for "gifts" on payday. This patient proposed that whenever John wanted to go to the hospital snack bar or store, he would go with him to assist; John readily accepted. While this type of caring behavior was not a specific goal of the study, it was observed as a healthy spin-off of the group-contingent reinforcement. It stands as striking evidence of the impact that can be achieved when group members are helped to see that they are interdependent on each other for accomplishing a shared goal.

Meaning-attribution is a leadership function that assumes increased importance in assisting the group to become more cohesive. It is the leader who should have both the perspective and the expertise to help the group members understand what they are doing together. The leader should point out the norm and value positions the group is developing, acknowledge with the group how difficult it is to change one's behavior or share feelings long-hidden from others, carefully follow the discussion themes that are developing in the group—whether they are working at avoiding conflict or deciding on restrictive solutions in their problem solving. In short, the leader should help them to make some sense out of their experiences in the group. This function of meaning-attribution will increase during the life of a healthy group.

THREATS TO GROUP COHESIVENESS

In my clinical experience, there are four major threats to group cohesiveness: unstable membership, group deviants, subgrouping, and leadership problems. Each interferes in its own way with the development or maintenance of group cohesiveness.

Unstable membership is a factor that is difficult to express in measurable or quantifiable terms. Given that groups vary along the dimensions of open or closed membership and open or closed time parameters, there is no available data on the degree of membership turnover that can be tolerated by different types of groups. The figure below illustrates the four possible combinations of time and membership variables. Research needs to be conducted on the types of group objectives that are best dealt with under each condition and the effects of membership turnover on each.

Membership

		Open	Closed
Time	Open	Norms—changing Goals—flexible	Norms—clear Goals—flexible
	Closed	Norms—changing Goals—specific	Norms—clear Goals—specific

In general it seems reasonable to hypothesize that the norms of the group are directly related to the stability of group membership, and the group goals are directly related to the time frame in which a group is functioning. This means that the norms of the group will vary as a function of how stable the group membership remains, while the group goals may vary as a function of the time in which the group has to work as a group. These hypotheses could be empirically tested.

The impact of unstable membership on the cohesiveness of the group could then be tested under each of the four conditions in the above figure. For now, I have to rely on clinical speculation and experience to explore the effects of unstable membership in each of the four quadrants.

When the group allows for both open membership and an unlimited number of sessions in which to work, it is likely that the goals will need to be flexible and the norms will change somewhat to accommodate new members if the group is to remain cohesive. In this type of group, rapid member turnover is a very real threat to group cohesion. I am reminded of the frustration of nurses on one acute inpatient ward as they attempted to develop group cohesion in their daily ward community meeting. The average length of stay for patients on their unit was just under 2 weeks, with most patients admitted in an acutely disturbed or psychotic condition. In addition, many of the nursing staff rotated shifts and students came and went during the course of the semester. What resulted was a group in which there were no norm-carriers—no one who stayed long enough to internalize a set of norms and gradually pass them on to new members. The goals of the group community meetings were constantly being questioned by and restated for new members. Because of its highly unstable membership, the group never became cohesive and was of questionable value to the patients and staff.

If the group leader is able to develop clear norms and specific goals, the group is more likely to survive some instability in membership. For example, a task group in which the members are planning ward activities is able to adjust assignments to include new members who will assume the tasks of discharged members. The less structured the activities of a group, the more important stable membership becomes. Groups in which there is a high level of interpersonal sharing will experience member turnover as more disruptive to their group process. When a group is planned for a set or closed period with an open membership, new members need to be selected more carefully for their ability to fit into the norms and goals of the group. For example, a 1-week series of discussion topics for newly diagnosed diabetic patients can accept a new member in the third session as long as that member is familiar with the information that was shared during the first two sessions. Otherwise, the group will be diverted from its goal as they attempt to update the new member.

It is often useful to structure a closed membership for time-limited groups. A nurse may plan a 5-session series of meetings with a group of 12-year-old girls to discuss grooming and physical appearance and develop a cohesive group very quickly. If one of the girls should happen to be discharged or leave the group before the planned sessions are over, her loss will be felt by the group. The remaining members may even be drawn closer together by sharing their reactions to her leaving. It is my experience that it is more functional to fulfill this time-limited commitment with a smaller group than to attempt to replace terminated members. The addition of new members is disruptive to the cohesiveness of the group.

Groups in which the time commitment is open but the membership is closed usually have difficulty in sustaining themselves. The gradual and naturally occurring loss of members eventually results in a decision to terminate the group. Most groups that do not work within a set time frame have some mechanism built-in for the inclusion of new members.

Group leaders should be aware of the effect of membership turnover on the cohesiveness of the group. A member leaving the group is a significant event. When new members join the group it is equally significant. Both events can be acknowledged and discussed within the group as a way of fostering cohesion. Both events, however, will have some impact on the norms and goals of the group. One group in which I was a co-leader confronted such a crisis when one of its older female members was discharged from the hospital. This woman had played the role of "nurturing mother" during her 5 months in the group and the younger group members clearly missed her. After several sessions in which the group devised multiple, unsatisfactory plans for dealing with their loss, they solved their problem by recruiting two new female members who had been recently admitted to the unit. They had found a way to preserve the integrity and cohesiveness of their group despite the loss of a significant member and assertively dealt with the selection of new members. The leaders were supportive of this group activity because of its positive effect on group cohesion.

Group deviants present a threat to group cohesiveness because of their variance from the norms and/or goals of the group. A deviant is someone who departs from or opposes the standards of the group. The following observations about the effect of deviants on health care groups are derived from my experience and the group dynamics research on laboratory and normal subjects. There is a need for research to test the applicability of these principles with health care groups.

Deviance is defined with respect to the norms and goals of the group. Thus in a task-oriented group someone who does not care about accomplishing the task or refuses to assume responsibility for their share of the work is considered deviant. Someone who gains weight is deviating from the goals of a weight-loss group, and a nonverbal member is clearly not following the group norms in a group that values open sharing of feelings.

In the chapter on selection of members for health care groups, the point was made that homogeniety of members should be viewed with respect to the norms and goals of the group, rather than demographic variables such as age, educational level, or diagnostic category. The importance of selecting members who subscribe to the norms of the group and are capable of participating in the achievement of group goals lies in their contribution to group cohesiveness. A group can often utilize unique input regarding ways of implementing its norms and goals much more readily than it can accept opposition to them. To date, no one has answered the question of how much deviance is too much deviance.

The group dynamics research is clear regarding the outcomes of group deviance.[14-16] Initially, considerable group effort and communication is directed to a deviant member if the group perceives there is a reasonable chance of changing his opinion or behavior. If, at some point, it becomes clear that the deviant cannot or will not change, communication toward him declines markedly. The group may redefine its boundaries so as to exclude the deviant member, and he might even be asked to leave.

Certain types of groups play a significant role in defining social reality for their members. Depending on how central the group is to its members' lives, the pressures exerted by the group toward uniformity may have significant impact on changing individual behavior. There is some evidence[17] to suggest that the group's tendency to reject the deviant is higher the more cohesive the group and the more central the deviance to the purposes of the group. Further,[25] high status members are allowed to deviate more from the group standards as long as their behavior is not detrimental to the group.[18] The group might even alter its norms and goals slightly so as not to exclude a high status member.

A health care group is more likely to become cohesive if the members have been selected for their ability to share the group norms and their willingness to subscribe to the goals of the group. Too much variance among members with respect to the group norms and goals may interfere with the group ever becoming cohesive. This is why, for example, attention should be given to the age and developmental level of young children when attempting to work with them in a group. Because of their different developmental capabilities, a 5 year old and a 10 year old do not share the same behavioral goals, nor should they be expected to engage in the same normative behavior within a group. The more important group cohesiveness is to the functioning of the group, the more attention should be paid to the selection of group members.

When a regular member of a health care group becomes a deviant with respect to a group issue, one of several events can occur. The group may exert considerable effort and energy toward this member in an attempt to foster conformity. For example, a hypertensive client who deliberately goes off his low-sodium diet may become the focus of an entire group effort to foster compliance with his health care regimen. Often the group concern and pressure will prompt a change in his behavior, and the group will become even more cohesive as a result of their mutual success in altering his behavior. If the group pressure is unsuccessful, the member may be ignored or even asked to leave the group. It is difficult for a group to include members who are not at least attempting to improve or maintain their health status because the threat to the integrity of the group is too great.

A unique form of group deviance/group cohesiveness can develop in groups whose membership is not voluntary. In some settings, group participation is required of mental patients, children, prisoners, or adolescents. The health professional who agrees to lead such a group should be alert to the potential of such groups for becoming cohesive around norms and goals that are not shared by the leader. In effect, the leader becomes the deviant with the group defining its boundaries in such a way as to exclude the leader and the leader's values. An example of one such group occurred in a residential treatment setting for adolescent girls. The girls had no choice about being hospitalized. Even though the group leaders offered their sex education group on a voluntary basis, they were dealing with group members who approached their health care from a rebellious rather than a voluntary stance. Further, the prevailing norm on the unit where the girls lived together was to act tough and not admit to fears and uncertainties regarding their lives. This meant that the group leaders had quite a challenge in determining just what information on human sexuality would be useful to the group. It was weeks before the members would even engage in any discussion that might reveal their lack of experience and knowledge with the reproductive system and sexual functioning. The group was very cohesive around the norm of laughing at information regarding sex and refusing to discuss issues with the leaders.

Subgrouping is another factor that can affect group cohesion. To some extent subgrouping is a result of the group's unwillingness or inability to resolve deviance regarding its norms and goals. Instead, one or several subgroups form naturally to support the behavioral differences of the members. Each subgroup may become very cohesive as it interferes with the cohesiveness of the entire group. Competition rather than cooperation may become the group norm with each subgroup supporting its own position and thereby protecting its existence.

Unless subgroups are task specific and time limited, they are actively discouraged by most small group leaders because of their devastating effect on the cohesiveness of the entire group. Some group leaders will discourage, or even forbid, social contact among members outside the group sessions, so that subgroups and restrictive norms are not developed. In other groups where the group norms and goals are more clearly defined, contact among members outside the group sessions is accepted or even encouraged. I have experienced numerous groups in which member contacts outside the group were extremely supportive and beneficial to the participants. If such contacts are part of the normative structure and supplement the goals of the group, they can be useful adjunct to health maintenance and change. Subgroups that detract from the cohesiveness of the total group, i.e., are not consistent with the norms and goals of the group, should be discouraged.

Finally, *leadership problems* can pose a serious threat to group cohesiveness. If the leader lacks the knowledge or ability to develop a cohesive group, the potential effectiveness of the group intervention will be compromised. Some leaders are inclined to keep the focus of the group's work and attention on themselves. They are the source of information and therapeutic interventions. I am aware of a number of leader-centered groups that have excellent client change outcomes. The point to be made here is that these leaders are not maximizing the potential benefits of working with clients in groups. On the other hand, there are many group leaders who rely solely on the interaction among group members to effect therapeutic change. These leaders do little more than convene the group and offer an occasional comment on the process that is occurring.

It is my opinion that the group leader is responsible for structuring and managing the process that takes place in health care groups. Through the careful planning of leader interventions and the shaping of member interactions, the group can be an extremely potent setting in which to deliver health care. Interventions that foster group cohesiveness will maximize the therapeutic potential of the health care group.

REFERENCES

1. Cartwright, D.: The nature of group cohesiveness. In Cartwright, D., and Zander, A. (eds.): New York, 1968, Harper & Row, Publishers.
2. Lieberman, M. A., Yalom, I. D., and Miles, M. B.: Encounter groups: First facts, New York, 1972, Basic Books.
3. Festinger, L.: Informal social communication. In Cartwright, D., and Zander, A. (eds.): Group dynamics, New York, 1968, Harper & Row, Publishers.
4. Yalom, I. D.: The theory and practice of group psychotherapy, New York, 1975, Basic Books, p. 45.
5. Dickoff, H., and Lakin, M.: Patients' views of group psychotherapy: Retrospections and interpretations, Int. J. Group Psychother. 13:61-73, 1963.
6. Kapp, F. T., et al.: Group participation and self-perceived personality change, J. Nerv. Ment. Dis. 139:255-265, 1964.
7. Yalom, I. D., Houts, P. S., and Zimerberg, S., and Rand, K. H.: Prediction of improvement in group therapy, Arch. Gen. Psychiatry 17:159-168, 1967.
8. Heider, F.: The psychology of interpersonal relations, New York, 1958, John Wiley & Sons, Inc.
9. Newcomb, T. M.: Varieties of interpersonal attraction. In Cartwright, D., and Zander, A. (eds.): Group dynamics, New York, 1968, Harper & Row, Publishers.
10. Festinger, L. A.: A theory of social comparison processes, Hum. Rel. 7:117-140, 1954.
11. Raven, Be. H., and Rietsema, J.: The effect of varied clarity of group goal and group path upon the individual and his relation to his group, Hum. Rel. 10:29-44, 1957.

12. Cartwright, D., and Zander, A. (eds.): Group dynamics, New York, 1968, Harper & Row, Publishers, p. 142.
13. Loomis, M. E.: Use of group contingencies with psychiatric patients, In ANA Clinical Sessions—1972, New York, 1973, Appleton-Century-Crofts, Inc.
14. Berkowitz, L., and Howard, R.: Reactions to opinion deviates as affected by affiliation need and group member interdependence, Sociometry 22:81-91, 1959.
15. Sampson, E. E., and Brandon, A.: The effects of role and opinion deviation on small group behavior, Sociometry 27:261-281, 1964.
16. Emerson, R.: Deviation and rejection: An experimental replication, Am. Soc. Rev. 19:688-693, 1954.
17. Schachter, S.: Deviation, rejection and communication. In Cartwright, D., and Zander, A. (eds.): Group dynamics, New York, 1968, Harper & Row, Publishers.
18. Wiggins, J. A., Dill, F., and Schwartz, R. D.: On "status-liability." In Cartwright, D., and Zander, A. (eds.): Group dynamics, New York, 1968, Harper & Row, Publishers.

8 □ The working phase of the group

Work is the activity by which a group accomplishes its goals. The working phase in the life of a health care group is characterized by active leader and member participation in accomplishing the goals and objectives of the group. While there are certainly problems and issues the group must confront during the working phase, a cohesive group is able to mobilize its collective problem-solving capabilities and resolve issues in a goal-oriented manner. This chapter will focus on a number of working issues commonly confronted by health care groups. The role of the leader and the curative factors that can be utilized to assist the group in its work will be explored in relation to the specific goals of the group.

The way in which a group accomplishes its goals and objectives can be viewed as differing along two important dimensions: content and process. A content-oriented group is one in which the majority of the group's time and energy is directed toward the actual substance or content of what is being said. A process-oriented group, on the other hand, attends much more to the way in which things are said, why they might have been said, and the timing and sequencing of member activities. The following figure illustrates the relationship between content and process in a variety of groups.

Groups can be located along a continuum from high-content, low-process to low-content, high-process emphasis. Task groups are the prototype of groups in which the majority of time and energy is devoted to content. If the task is to write bylaws for the organization, most of the member communication relates to deciding what committees the organization needs, what

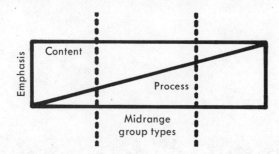

their membership should be, and which functions are appropriate for which committee. Roles will be based on the members' abilities to assist in the various subtasks necessary for accomplishing the objective. A clear-thinking, well-organized person will hopefully be selected to chair the group, and the tasks of collecting background information, writing, and public relations will be divided according to member interest and capabilities.

In its initial meetings, this bylaws committee will focus on process long enough to agree on norms regarding how they will accomplish their group goal. After that, the group will probably spend little if any time examining its process unless there is some internal or external interference with movement toward its goal. If a certain member is not meeting deadlines or the president of the organization (a noncommittee member) tries to tell the group which bylaws are important, the group will need to review and perhaps alter its process of working together. Theoretically, it is possible for a group to only deal with the content of its task and never attend to its process. In actual practice, this is seldom practical. As with this bylaws committee, there is usually some requirement that the group attend even minimally to the process by which it will accomplish its goals. Many efficient task groups, however, will spend 95% of their time and energy on the content of their task and only 5% of their time and energy on group process issues.

The other end of the content/process continuum is occupied by groups in which the process is continually scrutinized, almost to the exclusion of focusing on what is being said or done. Some psychotherapy groups and human relations training groups are in this category. In these groups great emphasis is placed on how and why people do what they do when they do it. A group member may ask a question that never gets answered because the other members will focus on why he cannot answer the question himself, how he asked for help, or what it means that all of the group members are asking questions today. Since very few health care groups utilize this much process orientation in accomplishing their objectives, this type of group will not be discussed in depth in this text.

Many health care groups utilize a blend of content and process that places them somewhere near the middle of the content/process continuum. The group leader, like a traffic control analyst in a helicopter, may hover low so as to fully attend to the content of what one person is saying. He may be asking for specific information about how to care for himself once he returns to work, and the group members share information from their own experiences. Later the leader may observe the group in a more general way and notice that all of the group members are avoiding expressing strong emotions or that the group seems to be frightened. In some groups individual change contracts are the focus of group activity and members in turn receive the individual attention of the group. Whatever the process/content orientation of the group, there are general issues with which most groups must deal during the working phase. These issues will be discussed from a combined content and process perspective.

RESISTANCE TO CHANGE

Most people experience some degree of difficulty when they set out to change an established behavior or feeling pattern. The old ways are familiar and predictable—even though painful at times—and there is a naturally occurring resistance to change. When the health professional is working with clients in a group, this natural resistance to change becomes a working issue for the entire group that may need to be dealt with any number of times. The following examples illustrate the ways in which resistance to change became apparent in several groups with different content/process orientations.

The first group was a support group in a community mental health center aftercare clinic. All eight of the group members had been hospitalized at least once for psychiatric problems ranging from severe depression to psychotic episodes. The clinic staff and the nurse who was the group leader felt that the group setting was the best vehicle for accomplishing their goals of support and prevention of further hospitalization for these clients. Most of the group members also attended the weekly medication clinic in the same agency since chemotherapy was seen as a useful component of their continued maintenance outside the hospital.

This particular group had been meeting weekly for 13 months with very little member turnover. Two of the members had been clients in the aftercare clinic since its inception 4 years earlier and provided a stable nucleus for clarifying the norms and goals of the clinic and their particular group to new group members. The group was clearly into the working phase and had a history of dealing effectively with a variety of resistances to change. The content of their weekly sessions generally focused on difficulties the members shared, such as relating to family members and friends, obtaining work with a record of hospitalization for emotional problems, and managing their anxiety around stressful or performance-related situations. While the nurse therapist of the group was aware of process issues as they occurred in the group, she chose to deal primarily with the content brought up in the sessions and assisted the group in problem solving about their difficulties.

In session 60, an old member, Frank, rejoined the group following a 1-month absence while he was an inpatient. Frank's hospitalization had been precipitated by an overt psychotic episode during which he lost his job and began wandering the streets in a delusional state. During Frank's absence, the other group members had expressed concern for his welfare and John and Mary had visited him once in the hospital.

The session in which Frank returned to the group was marked by numerous changes in the group's behavior. The members appeared anxious and had a great deal of difficulty discussing any one topic for more than 5 minutes. After an initial warm welcome for Frank, John and Mary led the group effort to ignore his presence. The therapist's attempts to include Frank in the discussion were circumvented by members talking with each other in diads and excluding both Frank and the therapist. By the end of the session, the therapist had angrily decided that it was her responsibility to take care of Frank since no one else seemed to care about him.

In session 61 the group actively engaged in a discussion of John's guilty feelings about being taken care of by his family as a result of his emotional problems. Various opinions were offered as to whether or not John should be feeling guilty. Once again, the group was clearly excluding Frank and the therapist from the discussion. When the therapist gently asked what she and Frank needed to do to be once again included in the group, the discussion stopped in shocked silence. The therapist then shared her awareness that the group members had some reactions to Frank's hospitalization and return to the group that they were avoiding. One by one, the other members began sharing their guilt about not noticing that Frank had been getting sicker and their fear that the same thing might happen to them. The group resistance to dealing directly with what had happened to Frank stemmed from their identification with his becoming psychotic and their anger at the therapist for letting it happen.

What evolved over the next several sessions was a very healthy and useful discussion of why Frank had decompensated and how that was similar to or different from what had happened to other group members. Frank shared with the group his secret decision to stop taking his medications because they made him sleepy at work and the subsequent return of his crazy thoughts. The therapist was able to reassure the group that they could not assume responsibility for the behavior of other members, especially when they lacked information about what the other person was doing. Gradually the group members also began to change their blanket acceptance of the social derogation they had experienced for being "mentally ill." They discussed situations in which their own presentation of themselves as being somehow inferior had helped to set up the interpersonal or professional rejection they had experienced. This awareness opened the way for finding new ways in which they could relate to family, friends, and co-workers.

The group leader was able to assist the group members in dealing with their resistance to acknowledging their feelings about Frank's rehospitalization because she was attentive to the overall process of the group. In addition to hearing the content of what was being said, she was also aware that the members were changing the topic frequently and ignoring Frank. When the leader attended to Frank, she too was excluded from the group. Her question of what she and Frank needed to do to be included in the group was designed to focus the members on the process that was occurring in the group. This confrontation was followed by supportive assistance from the leader as the members began to acknowledge their fear, anger, and guilt over Frank's rehospitalization. Both the confrontation and support were essential in assisting the group to deal with its resistance and work through this important issue.

The next example of resistance to change occurred in a group of adolescents hospitalized for chronic physical problems on a rehabilitation ward in a large children's hospital. Because of the normal, unpredictable schedule of admissions and discharges, the group membership was only moderately stable. The average length of stay on the unit was 2 months, and the group had an open membership policy to account for this pattern. The clinical nurse specialist who led the group described it to new members as a place where they could share common problems related to their physical conditions and work out plans for how they would manage their lives outside the hospital. The nurse herself was an expert in both adolescent development and in assisting youngsters to learn the activity modifications and self-care practices required by their physical limitations. The group met twice a week for 1 hour, and the content focus of the sessions varied greatly depending on the ages and physical conditions of the youngsters who attended. Some sessions were spent sharing information regarding physical care concerns such as bowel and bladder control, while other sessions foscused more generally on issues such as peer reactions to physical deformities.

Since the group membership varied from session to session, the clinical specialist maintained a very active role in interpreting the norms and goals of the group to the members. Group cohesiveness was enhanced by the ward living arrangement in which the youngsters were able to spend a great deal of their free time together. In this respect the health care group might be considered a subgroup of the larger group of adolescents on this rehabilitation unit where an atmosphere of caring and sharing existed.

Over the 2-month period prior to this example, the group membership had remained fairly constant. The youngsters had been actively involved in asking for and receiving information from each other and the nurse specialist. The sessions were filled with very active discussions regarding each member's various treatment procedures. The nurse was aware, however, of her growing discomfort over the impending discharge of two of the group members. As she thought about the source of her discomfort, she realized she was concerned that these two youngsters would not actually take care of themselves at home and would soon require rehospitalization. Further, as she observed the group members relating to the rest of the nursing staff on the ward, she noticed a certain degree of passivity. The youngsters were often the passive recipients of nursing care for treatment procedures that they were well able to administer to themselves.

At the next group session, the nurse shared her observations with the group. This disclosure was met with an initial volley of denials and disclaimers of any wrong-doing on the part of the members. "After all, nurses are supposed to take care of you; that's their job!" The leader persisted and shared her concern that unless the youngsters began accepting responsibility for the self-care practices of which they were capable, they might gradually accept a pattern of life in which most of their reinforcement and recognition came from being sick and cared for. What followed was a very active and sober discussion of the various adult possibilities of career, home, vacation, and family that were open to these youngsters despite their chronic illnesses.

For the next several sessions the members discussed the topic of assuming responsibility for their own behavior, feelings, and the course of their lives in general. Each of them actively implemented plans for managing more of their own care in the hospital in preparation for home passes and eventual discharge. The nurse specialist also worked with the ward nursing staff and the youngsters' family members to make sure that their newfound independence would be monitored and reinforced. What began as a group resistance to change evolved into a rewarding growth experience as these adolescents and their families accomplished an important developmental task together. The nurse specialist was able to utilize her knowledge of adolescent growth and development, nursing care of chronic conditions, and group process to influence this change.

The final example of resistance to change is generalizable to most groups in which specific behavior change is the primary objective. In groups that have been formed to help members quit smoking, lose weight, or learn social skills, the members share a uniform or common focus of concern. The group leader usually has a fairly specific program for assisting the members to change and works with the assumption that members would not be attending the group if they were not motivated to change a specific behavior.

When resistance to change becomes a working issue in the group, it is usually because one, several, or all of the members have a high investment in the old behavior that they are having difficulty relinquishing. For example, in a weight-loss group the members are required to drastically alter their eating behaviors. This may mean giving up food as a primary source of reinforcement or comfort, changing social relationships such as going out for a late evening dinner after bowling, and altering one's self-concept from that of a fat, jolly person. Even if one is committed to losing weight, the changes associated with weight loss require abandoning safe and predictable patterns for new and less comfortable behaviors. This ambivalence is what resistance is all about.

A group resistance occurs when group members share a common resistance to change and reinforce each other for not changing. More often than not the group leader becomes aware of a group resistance by attending to what is *not* being said or a change that is *not* occurring. As in the previous two examples, the group members were not aware of their resistance until it was articulated and confronted by the leader. They were merely doing what most people do—avoiding a source of discomfort.

In a group whose objective is behavior change, the obvious time to question the presence of group resistance is when the desired change is not occurring. This lack of change often takes the form of one or several members not changing and the rest of the group either ignoring or reinforcing the lack of change. In this situation the group leader is aided by the presence of an initial, clear contract for group participation. If new members have been prepared for group and have made a clear commitment to participate in the goals and norms of the group, then lack of change is a deviation from that contract. The contract serves as the guide against which behavior change or lack thereof can be measured.

In my experience, there are several guidelines for dealing with group resistance. The leader first needs to become aware of a behavior pattern that has developed. The behavior needs to be clear enough that the group members will recognize it when it is pointed out. For instance, the leader may notice that several of the group members have not met their goal of reducing their cigarette smoking by five cigarettes the previous week. When nobody in the group initially comments on this occurrence, the leader may decide to wait a while and let the group process develop before intervening. The group may talk superficially for a while or several other members may lead the group in a discussion questioning the value of the group. Once it has become clear that the group is going to ignore the difficulties experienced by the two members, a behavior pattern has emerged. The leader might then question the meaning of the preceding discussion by saying something like, "I wonder if there's a connection between questioning the value of the group and the fact that Fred and Lois have not met their smoking goals for this week."

It is important that this issue be raised as an inquiry and not as an accusation, so that the group is encouraged to examine the meaning of its own behavior. People are not likely to examine and then change behaviors about which they are feeling defensive. The key to change in this situation is confrontation coupled with support. This means that the leader must confirm the situation with the group, capture their interest in exploring its meaning, and assist them in moving toward resolution or change. In terms of the leadership roles previously defined, this will require a decrease in executive functioning, a moderate to high dose of stimulation, a high level of caring, and a high reliance on the leader for meaning-attribution.

If the leader believes that all behavior has meaning, the group can be assisted to explore both sides of the ambivalence involved in its resistance. Consider the previously mentioned group that wanted to quit smoking. On a personal level, Fred and Lois are having difficulty giving up a behavior (smoking) that they realize is harmful but which has served some function for them. Similarly, the other group members are also working to alter a behavior that has given them some degree of satisfaction and lends a certain structure to their activities. For some members, giving up smoking may even mean giving up a decision to be disabled or even die from lung cancer.

To quit smoking will therefore involve making a new decision to live and be healthy.

On a group level, the norms and goals of the group have been violated by Fred's and Lois' not meeting their objectives. If this is an infrequent occurrence, the working-phase group is likely to be cohesive enough to handle this deviance by mobilizing group pressures to uniformity. If this is a frequent occurrence, or if Fred and/or Lois are influential group members, the norms and goals of the group have been threatened. It is this threat to the integrity of the group that must be explored as a group maintenance issue. The working-phase group can be asked how they feel when influential members have difficulty in meeting group expectations—what this means to each of them individually and about the group collectively. What follows is likely to be a discussion of the fear, anger, and group pressures that are experienced in this and similar situations. As the members share their concerns and wishes for themselves and each other, a renewed commitment to the group—its norms and goals—will emerge. The working through of group resistances inevitably results in a more cohesive group.

CLOSENESS

In the context of this discussion, closeness is the ability to make contact—contact with oneself or with another person. It requires being in the here and now, tuned into oneself and aware of one's unique feelings and existence. When closeness involves another person, it requires a commitment to honest communication on both their parts. Closeness between two people often means engaging in an intimate struggle to understand and be understood. While periods of closeness can be enjoyed for brief moments, the concept usually implies an ongoing relationship over some period during which open sharing occurs.

For most people in today's western cultures, closeness is a relatively unique experience. As people are socialized into family, school, or career, they gradually discard some portion of their natural spontaneity for the more structured, stereotyped requirements of a given role. Each role a person plays, be it wife, mother, nurse, husband, business executive, high school dropout, or neighborhood "good Joe," has an expected repertoire of behaviors, feelings, and relationship patterns. In addition, if one plays the role correctly, other people tend to respond in a predictable manner. Eventually, all of the actors engaged in this prearranged drama have learned to exchange predictable quantities of recognition and reinforcement. The bank executive who responds to a peak work period by volunteering to come in and work on the weekend is rewarded while a counterpart who refuses to work more than a 60-hour week to spend time with the family will find advancement within the organization difficult.

To meet the expectations of their various roles, many people deny certain aspects of themselves. They may actually lose touch with what they really want or feel in certain situations. If a good mother is supposed to place the needs of her family first, it becomes difficult for her to take her own feelings into account. Even if she is aware of being tired or angry at her children, she may feel guilty and attempt to hide these "unacceptable" feelings. Both denial and guilt over some aspect of oneself make it extremely difficult if not impossible to be close.

As mentioned in Chapter 1, a health care group often provides people with the unique experience of making contact with themselves and other human beings. Frequently the roles with which a person is familiar are not the same roles that are reinforced in the group. People who run large businesses are suddenly assuming the role of students in learning about their pacemakers. Women who have assumed that their job was to care for others are accepting nurturing, while men who learned to be brave and strong are reinforced for having and expressing their feelings. And since the issues being dealt with are very basic, human ones, it is best that people not play roles. What then emerges is an experience of closeness and sharing that can be a very unique experience for some group members.

Closeness was mentioned as an issue of "near or far" in Chapter 6. It is also an ongoing issue with which most groups must deal during the working phase. Like cohesiveness, closeness is one of those variables that is both a cause and an effect. A certain degree of closeness and honest sharing is required for the members to feel safe to work on important issues in the group. However, once sharing has occurred among the members and the group has been supportive and helpful, closeness is enhanced.

In setting the stage for closeness and direct sharing within the group, the leader must be aware of developing a group environment that is protective and safe. The group norms must be such that people are not discounted— that people and their feelings are acknowledged and respected. Perhaps the best method for developing this norm is the role-modeling that is done by the leader. The caring function of the group leader will set the tone for the group members and communicate a safe environment. Direct statements by the leader are sometimes necessary. "I expect that we will challenge as well as listen to each other, but it is not acceptable to discount or ignore each other's feelings or behavior."

There has been so much publicity about encounter groups and new human potential experiences since the mid-1960s, that some people are wary when asked to participate in a health care group. Some potential clients will ask directly if this is a "touchy-feely" group or if they will be expected to roll around on the floor and scream. Others will just look uncomfortable and graciously decline. As has been pointed out earlier, it is important to answer all questions about the group clearly and directly. If the expression and sharing of feelings is part of the group format, this should be acknowledged. People for whom the sharing of feelings currently imposes too great a risk will usually keep themselves out of such a group.

Closeness is a state that is usually enhanced by the sharing of common experiences. During the working phase, the leader and group members work together at solving the problems or meeting the objectives that have been defined as the purpose of the group. As cohesiveness develops through the sharing of common norms and goals and the members begin to feel safe with each other and the leader, a feeling of closeness is also developing. Once the group has actually been able to help some of the members, they will identify with the group and feel close to each other.

This is where the sharing of common experiences and similar affective states is so important. For example, a task-oriented group that has worked together to solve a mutually agreed on problem is sharing a common experience. During the course of their work together, the group members are likely to have similar feelings of frustration at the complexity of the problem, anger at a member's not getting his work done on time, pleasure over a humorous situation, and pride, relief, and joy at the eventual completion of the task. With each of these shared experiences, comes closeness. The group members do not even have to see or like each other outside the group. If they are committed to struggling together on the group problem, eventually a sense of group identity and closeness will emerge.

The same is true in groups whose format is the sharing of personal situations. I am reminded of a group for spouses of myocardial infarction patients that appeared to be going along quite smoothly over a number of sessions. The members were discussing many of their concerns regarding activity, dietary, and family adjustments that would need to be made once their spouses returned home. They shared their own experiences and solutions willingly and were generally attuned to each other's problems. In one session Mr. Fredricks, a 64-year-old business executive whose wife was hospitalized in the Coronary Care Unit, failed to appear and had not informed anyone of his intended absence. The group members wondered where he was, decided he must still be at the office, and went on with the usual business of planning for their spouses' return home.

About halfway through the session, Mr. Fredricks appeared in the doorway, tears streaming down his cheeks. He had just come from the C.C.U where his wife had suffered a second and more severe coronary and died. The group was stunned. The sight of this usually composed man openly experiencing the pain of his loss touched everyone in the room. Some members cried; others embraced Mr. Fredricks as he told them he had come to the group because he did not know where else to go. The group met for an extra hour that night as Mr. Fredricks alternately reminisced and expressed his sorrow over the loss of his wife. He told of their retirement plans, their past joys, and the future they would never share. Gradually the group helped him to make plans for the next several days and made certain that he had a support system he could use during the week until the group met again.

The group left the hospital together that night and remained emotionally close in the sessions that followed. They had shared a common grief that bonded them together in a new way. Other members were able to discuss their own fears of loss and abandonment that had been brought to awareness through Mr. Fredricks' experience. They learned how to ask for help and trust that others would care about them. Most importantly they learned in their closeness how to struggle with life in the face of death and move through their fears.

Not every group has such poignant, life-and-death issues with which to deal. However, the direct sharing of feelings within the group is a common precursor of closeness. There are many variations on the basic feelings of sad, mad, glad, or scared that are experienced in working groups. What the members gain from this experience may vary. Generally speaking, they learn that it is okay to have their feelings, to seek out an environment in which it is safe to express them, to trust that they will be responded to directly by caring people, and to know that they will feel better following an experience of closeness.

The importance of the group leader in structuring an environment that is. protective of the group members has already been mentioned. Very few people will risk the self-disclosure involved in directly sharing their feelings unless they feel safe. A high level of caring on the part of the leader is essential.

Stimulation is a leadership function that can be utilized in moderate doses to promote caring. There are times when it is extremely useful for leaders to share their feelings and reactions with the group as a way of encouraging members to express their feelings. Leaders should remain sensitive to the timing of this intervention and the response of group members. If the leader is afraid and withdraws from the expression of feelings, the group members are very likely to do the same. If, on the other hand, the leaders themselves or other members are allowed to flood the room with feelings, the group is not likely to feel safe.

Regardless of the level of feeling and closeness being expressed, it is important that the leader remain aware of the meaning-attribution function. If the members are helped to cognitively understand what they have experienced in the group, they will be in a much better position to utilize their experience in other situations. It is my experience that people can learn to think and feel at the same time. People who have previously learned to isolate their feelings from their thoughts will need some assistance in reintegrating these functions. A caring leader who uses moderate stimulation and a high level of meaning-attribution can be of great assistance with this process.

CONFLICT

The presence of divergent opinions or feelings can produce a conflict situation. At times people experience conflict internally as when a student nurse wants to visit friends but knows that an exam is scheduled for the next day. The student can resolve this internal conflict in a variety of ways. The student can decide to visit the friends and not prepare for the exam. The student can leave the friends and go home to study. A compromise can be worked out for meeting both objectives such as staying to visit for an hour and then studying, or studying with the friends. The visit can be delayed until after the exam. If there is extreme conflict about the seemingly incompatible goals, the nurse can ask the friends for help in deciding.

How the student resolves this conflict situation will depend on several factors. Some of these are past experience with similar situations, the importance of the exam, the student's perception of the level of preparation for the exam, the importance of spending time with the friends, and the expectation of negative consequences for either not visiting or not studying. For example, if the friends are moving across the country the next morning, the student might decide to spend the evening with them and ask the instructor for permission to delay taking the exam. There are obviously numerous complex options for resolving this relatively simple conflict situation.

A similar but even more complex type of conflict can occur between two or more people in a group setting. The more people with divergent opinions or feelings who are involved in a conflict, the more potentially complex it becomes. Within a group, conflict can occur between two members, between subgroups of members, and between the leader and members. The issues around which conflict can occur generally relate to the objectives of the group, the way in which the group is structured, the roles of the leader and members, the group goals and norms, or the outcomes of group functioning. Conflict can also occur on a continuum ranging from mild disagreement to open hostility.

Regardless of the issue that is the focus of the conflict, the process by which the leader and members deal with the conflict is of paramount importance. A disagreement between members can be avoided, resolved constructively, or exaggerated to the point at which it destroys group functioning. Examples of member, subgroup, and leader–member conflicts will be used to illustrate methods of constructive conflict resolution in the working-phase group.

A subgroup conflict had been gradually developing in an ongoing weight-loss group in a storefront free peoples' clinic. Four of the eight young members had been religiously following their diets and behavior modification plans. As each of the four met their weekly goals for weight loss and dietary change, they gradually formed a mutually reinforcing subgroup and began enjoying each other's company outside the group. Their association contained many positive elements that assisted them in accomplishing the self-concept changes required by their weight loss. They enjoyed exchanging stories of their new dating experiences and shared shopping expeditions for stylish clothing and cosmetics.

This subgroup's transition from "fat" to "thin" was made more obvious by the presence of four newer group members who were having difficulty losing weight. In the weekly group meetings these four women sat by and sullenly watched the progress of the "thinning" subgroup. Their envy turned into anger one session when Lisa, the "leader" of the thin subgroup, began to snicker over the reported weight gain of Mary, one of the newer members. As the leader watched silently, the subgroups engaged in a series of verbal volleys that seemed to clear the air. The thin subgroup accused the newer members of not trying, while the new subgroup banded to gether to prove how nonsupportive the thin group had been.

During the silence that followed, the leader thought through her various options for constructive resolution of the conflict. She had no desire to see the two subgroups remain separate, since this would consume much of the group's time and energy and detract from their primary goal of weight loss. On the other hand, the group contract did not include a process orientation of examining interpersonal conflict and exploring the origins of competition within the group. As the leader shared these thoughts with the group, she clearly stated her objective that the two subgroups learn to cooperate, for they had much to learn from each other. She then proposed a method for beginning where the group was and moving them to a more cooperative position.

The subgroups willingly agreed to a weekly contest in which the total improvement or weight loss scores of two teams would be compared. The winners would then be treated to lunch at a local health food restaurant. Because of the wide variance in the weights of the group members, the teams were matched as closely as possible with respect to current weights and desired weights of team members. This necessitated forming teams that crossed established subgroups.

As the weekly competitions progressed, what emerged was a friendly rivalry and very close scores between the two teams. The leader was able to capture the competitive spirit and use it to the entire group's advantage. In addition, with the disruption of the subgroups and the weekly total group lunches, a new atmosphere of sharing and cooperation emerged. The eight members learned to understand and respect each other's differences as well as their similarities.

In the above example, the conflict that developed between the two subgroups was the result of differences between member norms. Even though the entire group subscribed to the goal of weight loss, each subgroup was attempting to meet that goal in a slightly different way. Eventually the thin subgroup also evolved some additional socialization goals for their group. The subgroup of newer members who were having difficulty losing weight was seen as a threat to the cohesiveness of the thin subgroup and was therefore excluded as deviant. The group leader utilized her awareness of group process in planning her interventions. She perceived that group competition as it had evolved and group cooperation were mutually exclusive processes. Her plan to use the competition to move the entire group to a more cooperative posture was clever and effective. She included the group in her planning, but clearly exercised her executive function as group leader to effect the change. She assumed a neutral position regarding the expression of envious and angry feelings—neither encouraging nor discouraging them. Her level of caring about all the group members was obvious as she refused to be drawn into each subgroup's discounting of the other. She explained what needed to be done and then facilitated the accomplishment of goals for the entire group.

When the working-phase group singles out an individual member as the object of conflict, chances are there is an unresolved issue—usually related to the leader—with which the group is not dealing. This phenomenon of redirecting conflicts away from their original source is called "scapegoating." Scapegoating often occurs when the real object of the conflict is perceived as being too powerful to confront directly. The group leader is in a position of reward and punishment as well as expert, legitimate, and referent power in most groups. It is no wonder that most group members experience some hesitation in confronting the leader directly.

For example, the medical director of a small outpatient psychiatric clinic persisted in arriving late for staff meetings. The rest of the staff adjusted to his lateness by either coming late themselves or socializing until the director arrived. This situation had persisted over 6 months of biweekly staff meetings before there was any obvious cause for concern. The staff had been preparing for a Blue Cross audit of the client records when they realized that one of the psychologists, Charles, was behind in recording his group progress notes. Despite Charles' promises that he would have his files complete in time for the audit, the group persisted in trying to "help" him with his "record-keeping problem." After several meetings in which he—and by implication anyone else who let their progress notes slip—was the focus of attention, Charles finally called a halt to the group scapegoating. He pointed out that something else must be going on with the group for so much to be made of his "problem" that he was already in the process of correcting.

In this situation it was not until some months later under the guidance of an outside consultant that the staff group finally acknowledged their anger at the medical director for his inattentiveness to the clinic staff. It took the assistance and safety of an uninvolved expert for this professional staff group to confront the real conflict issue. Because the director was willing to acknowledge, examine, and alter his own behavior, the entire clinic staff was able to move through this conflict to arrive at a more productive working relationship.

A number of the variables from this example are common to conflict situations within groups. Scapegoating of members has already been referred to as a phenomenon that occurs when the real conflict is perceived as too threatening to deal with directly. In this situation the issue for which Charles was being scapegoated—his inattentiveness to the details of caring for his clients' records—was similar to the issue over which the staff was angry at the director—his inattention to his job of caring for the staff and clinic. There is often a common theme between the scapegoating issue and the hidden conflict issue.

The need for an external, expert consultant to facilitate conflict resolution among the clinic staff points up several important principles. First, the group needed to feel safe and be assured of protection in confronting the leader. In many health care groups the prospect of confronting the expert leader of the group and risking the loss of the leader's caring is too threatening for the group to do unassisted. The leader needs to give permission for this confrontation to occur and ensure the members' protection. In this example, the director gave his permission by bringing in a consultant. In other groups this permission and protection is afforded by the presence of a co-leader who can actively assist the group in dealing with the conflict.

Secondly, if the leader is the source or object of the conflict, he or she is likely to be unaware of the importance or impact of his or her own behavior on the group. It is invariably most difficult for people, even group leaders, to examine their own behavior objectively. In our clinic example, this objective appraisal was provided by the external consultant. It can also be provided by a good co-leader or by a skilled group process supervisor. Many clinicians prefer to work with a co-leader and/or obtain group process supervision for just this reason. Objective appraisal of the group process and the leader's role with respect to the group is essential to a productive group.

When scapegoating occurs, it needs to be examined as a probable symptom of underlying leadership conflict. The issue around which the group is scapegoating may appear very reasonable. In the above example, Charles had not kept his progress notes up to date. This was a fact he readily admitted. However, when he made plans for correcting the situation and shared them with the group, he was virtually ignored. The group appeared to be more interested in the process of scapegoating than in the resolution of the ostensible issue. This is a sign that something else is going on, as Charles eventually pointed out. In this case, the "something else" was scapegoating.

Conflict involving the leader, either indirectly through scapegoating, or directly through member confrontation is among the most difficult situations for leaders to manage. Because of personal involvement, it is difficult, if not impossible, for the leader to remain objective in the assessment of the thoughts and feelings being expressed. The difficulty is expressed in the following internal dialogue. "Maybe they're right. Maybe I haven't been supportive enough of the progress people are making. On the other hand, at least half the group has trouble taking in any positive comments I make. Maybe it's all their problem and I should confront them with it. I don't know what to do. Sure am glad I have supervision tomorrow!"

The group leader need not struggle alone with such problems. As has been mentioned, co-leaders can provide a valuable source of moderately objective input. Also, good supervision of group process is invaluable, and outside consultants can sometimes be made available. However, the most obvious source of assistance that many group leaders neglect to consider are the group members themselves. On numerous occasions, I have sensed that something is going on—an unresolved conflict within the group—and have asked the group directly for input. "Why are we having trouble working together?" is one such question; or "Help me figure out why we seem stuck." Rather than guessing at the problem, the leader and group can work together toward problem identification and solution.

Engaging the group in the identification and resolution of process problems encourages a spirit of cooperation rather than competition. There is no such thing as a leadership problem or members' problem. Within a working group there are only group problems. If the members or leader are in conflict or competing with each other, there is a group problem, and group problems can only be solved cooperatively if the group is to remain an interdependent unit. Conflicts need to be resolved eventually and that is the work of the entire group.

WORKING THROUGH

Work is the activity by which a group accomplishes its goals. A group that has been structured clearly and that has developed a high level of group cohesiveness is in an excellent position to deal with issues that develop during the working phase. It is able to mobilize its collective problem-solving capabilities and resolve issues such as resistance to change, closeness, and group conflict in a goal-oriented manner. The resolution of these and other working-phase issues on the part of the group constitutes working through.

Working through occurs in all types of groups. A content-oriented group such as a task group works through issues that arise as it attempts to accomplish its goal. For example, the task of the ward improvement committee on an adolescent inpatient unit was to work with the staff to improve the physical appearance of the unit. The committee began its work by clarifying its potential resources and sphere of authority with the unit administrator. They raised questions such as: Who had final approval over any plans that they developed? To whom were they to propose certain changes? How much money did they have to work with? Could they plan activities for raising funds for their projects? Would the unit staff assist them in involving the other youngsters on the unit in various projects?

The next task of the committee was to specify and operationally define its goals. Exactly what was meant by improving the physical appearance of the unit? The answer to this question took the form of behaviorally specific objectives such as paint the game room, make curtains for the windows, initiate a room clean-up campaign among all the youngsters on the unit, clean the carpeting, decorate the corridors with graphics, make slipcovers for the dayroom furniture, and other similar projects.

During the course of defining these objectives and devising plans for accomplishing them, the committee had numerous problems to solve. They had to divide work within the committee and develop roles and patterns of communication among themselves. They had to resolve differences of opinion over what colors and fabrics should be selected and conflicts over who would do which tasks. They had to develop norms for how they would work together once a specific project was selected and deal with both "bossy" and "lazy" committee members. The working through process of the committee involved addressing and resolving each of these issues as they emerged in the work of the committee.

As with most such groups in health care settings, the nursing staff who were working with the youngsters had several parallel objectives for the committee. They definitely wanted to improve the physical appearance of the unit. In addition, they wanted these adolescents to learn some of the age-appropriate behaviors involved with the specific projects such as sewing, painting, raising money, and assuming responsibility for their environment. The staff also wanted the committee to learn to work together as a group and solve problems in a goal-directed manner. Over the 2 years of the committee's work, these youngsters worked through and learned to handle a great many issues that they would also be confronting in their lives outside the hospital as they moved from adolescence to adulthood.

The process of working through is not always a straight line process leading from problem identification to problem resolution and good feelings. Often a group will get bogged down in its goal-directed activities and not know why. They simply know that they have stopped being productive. They may talk about this lack of productivity for a while and decide, for example, that the members have too many other pressures impinging on their time and the group should meet less often. This may or may not be the solution to the group's difficulty. In fact, the group may go through this cycle of bogging down, figuring out why, and making the necessary changes any number of times. One such committee involved in a complex hospital planning process spent a whole year spinning its wheels and attempting to adjust its method of working together until it finally realized that its charge from the hospital director was sufficiently vague as to ensure that the committee got nothing done. The relief experienced by the committee members was enormous as they were about initiating a dialogue with the director to clarify their charge. As they worked through this issue, all the members experienced renewed energy. Relief and renewed energy are often signs that a group has worked through a problem issue.

This same cycle from problem identification to potential solution and back to problem clarification, leading to eventual working through and resolution is also characteristic of more process-oriented groups. The group may move through a series of incomplete or restrictive solutions before arriving at a resolution that will enable it to progress with its work. A support group for single parents provides a good example of this process. This group was developed by a public health nurse for the purpose of providing practical assistance, emotional support, and interpersonal contact for single parents who had to confront the dual job of supporting and parenting a family without the assistance of a spouse. The weekly group meetings were spent helping members to solve day-to-day problems such as child care, missing work when a youngster is sick, how to make ends meet on a small income, and providing children with contact with adults of both sexes. The group developed a very cohesive, supportive atmosphere in which the members could share the joys and frustrations of raising children.

One theme that predictably emerged was the question of marriage. The group dealt with the marriage theme from many different angles: the importance of marriage, the decline of nuclear families in today's society, the value of multiple versus monogamous relationships, and the importance of a mother and father for young children while they are growing up. During these discussions, the group arrived at a series of temporary solutions to the question of marriage. Their initial discussion ended with the angry conclusion that society places far too much emphasis on the institution of marriage for social status and economic stability. The next time the issue was discussed, the group acknowledged that marriage or remarriage might be worth considering for the benefit of their young children. Finally, 4 months after the issue was first discussed, the members were able to admit their feelings of anger, guilt, and sadness at not being married. Once these feelings were expressed by each member, the group was able to move on to a consideration of the various options each member had for structuring their personal lives.

While a group is working through any single issue, other work is also occurring. In fact, a number of group themes or working issues can be at different stages of resolution simultaneously. Within a single session the group might work on their feelings about marriage, help one of the members plan a study schedule for final exams taking his children's needs into consideration, and then share some of the parental joys of watching their youngsters develop. Across sessions, the work of the group can be compared to a complex filing system. A file or working issue may be pulled from the shelf for a time while the group is working on it. The issue may then be reshelved and not attended to for several sessions while the group works on other issues.

It is the job of the leader to attend to the issues or group themes that are on the table and being actively dealt with, how many have been shelved with incomplete or restrictive solutions, and which issues can be comfortably placed in the inactive file. (No group theme or issue is ever "dead." A new member or an important event in the group may call for an issue that has been resolved to be reopened and worked on once again.) The leader will need to pay close attention to the timing of reintroducing unresolved issues. If the issue is central to the functioning of the group, such as trust among the members, the leader may need to remind the group at regular intervals that the difficulties they are experiencing seem to relate to their lack of commitment to open sharing. Unresolved issues have a way of re-emerging in the group discussions. If the leader is alert to which issues are on the shelf awaiting resolution, the group can be moved into dealing with the appropriate working issue when the opportunity presents itself.

The process of working through group issues involves the use of a number of the curative factors presented in Chapter 3. As the chart on p. 42 illustrates, the importance of each of the curative factors seems to depend on the objectives of the group. This difference among types of groups is especially true during the working phase. A support group will rely heavily on the factors of group cohesiveness, altruism, and the imparting of information to get the job done. Socialization groups are primarily concerned about the development of socializing techniques and group cohesiveness during the working phase. The primary curative factor in human relations training groups is interpersonal learning, with group cohesiveness, catharsis, imitative behavior, and the imparting of information having a lesser, but significant function. In learning–behavior change health care groups, the imparting of information is extremely important during the working phase. Group members usually need information about their health care situation and the changes that are expected of them to be able to work in the group. As with other groups, the factor of group cohesiveness is a prerequisite to the groups' working together as well as a curative factor affecting behavior change. There is a certain degree of structured task orientation as the group works on the objective of losing weight, learning to care for their colostomies, or other similar health related behaviors. Imitative behavior and altruism are also important factors affecting the work of the group.

All the curative factors are important in psychotherapy groups; however, Yalom[1] places special emphasis on group cohesiveness and interpersonal learning. During the working phase of the group catharsis, imitative behavior, the imparting of information, the development of socializing techniques, and altrusim can all be factors that assist the group with its work. Some more process-oriented therapy groups rely heavily on the recreation of the primary family within the group setting and the group is used as a microcosm of the member's larger world. The corrective handling of issues within the group is of curative value as the leader and members refuse to relate to each other in stereotyped, unproductive ways. While universality is important during the initial stage of the group, the working group must eventually acknowledge the existential factors that account for each member's unique feelings, behaviors, thoughts, and personal responsibilities.

In summary, the leader of any health care group must assist the group in confronting and resolving issues during the working phase. Depending on the objectives of the group, a variety of curative factors are available to the leader. While the group members are often capable of assisting in the work of the group, it remains the responsibility of the leader to recognize and monitor the working themes and issues within the group. From a position of caring, the leader must firmly guide the group toward constructive resolution of such issues as resistance to change, closeness, and conflict. When the work of the group is capably managed, the leader and members alike will experience the relief and renewed energy of working through.

REFERENCE

1. Yalom, I. D.: The theory and practice of group psychotherapy, New York, 1975, Basic Books.

9 □ Termination in groups

Termination is an important event in the life of health care groups. It is an event that signifies the reality of death in the presence of life. Depending on the circumstances surrounding individual or group terminations, the event can take on the significance of a graduation or a funeral. Indeed, the ending of relationships within the group, like so many other group events, can be viewed as a microcosm of experiences in the larger world.

Many people avoid experiencing the joy of closeness and the pain of loss that are an unrecognized part of leave-takings in today's highly mobile, transient society. Graduation parties, wedding showers, and boisterous farewell parties can all be used to avoid dealing with the reality of relationships that are ending or changing. How many people can remember the promises to write and visit that are made by high school seniors on their way to colleges scattered across the country? And then there was the sad and empty feeling that came sometime within the next year or two when the old gang tried to get together over a vacation break and re-experience their past closeness, only to find that the relationships had changed. The fantasy of never saying good-bye is difficult to implement, and each person is left to deal with their sadness and loss alone.

The leader of a health care group is responsible for assisting the group members to deal with termination issues. Beginning with the initiation of a health care contract, termination should be a reality in the life of the group. If the group is time limited with a set number of sessions, this reality is a part of the initial contract. The knowledge of an ending point serves as a time measure against which the leader and members can pace their work. If the group is open ended with members leaving and entering at irregular intervals, each member's contract for work in the group should include a clear definition of what they intend to accomplish and how they will know when they have met their objectives. This contract can be renegotiated any number of times as members work in the group, but their objectives should always be clear. Ideally this clarity will assist both members and leader to know when their work in the group is finished.

In some settings, there are support groups that have no clear criteria for termination. I am familiar with aftercare groups in some community mental health and state hospital settings where the objectives are stated in terms of support and prevention of hospitalization. The leaders of these groups experience some difficulty in knowing when members no longer need the group. Generally speaking, in this type of situation it is wise to attend to the feelings of both the client and the group leader. Eventually, the client may grow disinterested in the group sessions. The group is no longer viewed as the focal point of the client's week, but rather as an obligation that must be met. Concomitantly, the leader may begin wondering what the group is doing to help this person. He seems to be doing fine on his own. Both client and leader should recognize the possible meaning of these thoughts and discuss the client's changing needs for the group's support within the group setting. It may be that termination is indicated or a less frequent schedule of group attendance might be desirable. In some settings where long-term outpatient care is indicated, clients never officially leave the group unless they move from the area. They are always free to attend the aftercare group when the need arises.

In most health care groups, termination can occur in one of two ways. Either the entire group terminates or an individual member or leader leaves the group. While each of these types of termination will be discussed in detail, the general approach is still the same. Termination of any sort is an extremely important event in health care groups. It should be recognized, explored, and resolved much as any other working issue in the group. Regardless of the type of termination, people need to say good-bye.

Just as the death of a relative or close friend usually prompts people to reflect on their own mortality, so group members reflect on the meaning of their individual and collective activities when a member leaves the group. Individual members may utilize this event to review their own progress in the group. Whether the member leaving was successful in meeting his objectives for group membership or not, the event often prompts comparisons among the remaining members. How are they doing in the group? Have they made as much progress as Mr. X who is leaving? In what ways are they similar or dissimilar to the leaving member?

Likewise, the potency of the group in helping people is brought into question when members leave. Did we help him or not? Are we an effective group? Will the group help me? Thus, individual members and the group as a whole use the termination experience to reflect on life.

When a member leaves because he has accomplished his objectives for being a group member, the response of the group is generally very positive. The other members will usually identify with the successful client and enjoy the feeling that they too can be successful in the group. Occasionally a member who is determined to not make it in the group will resent the successful member. Most often, however, members find it more desirable to identify with other members who have met the goals and subscribed to the norms of the group.

When a successful member leaves, the group as a potent vehicle for assistance and change is reaffirmed. The leaving member usually thanks everyone for their help, the group underscores how much the individual has changed, and their mutual pleasure fills the room. By the same token, an unsuccessful group member who leaves, can arouse fear on the part of individual members that they too will be unsuccessful and can shake the omnipotence of the group in general.

I am reminded of two leave-takings from the same psychotherapy group that occurred several months apart. In the first instance, Donna, a young wife and career woman, was leaving the group to accept a job in another city. She had only been in the group for 7 months, but during that time had demonstrated a remarkable determination and ability to deal directly with her treatment issues. Given her initial high level of anxiety and lack of psychological sophistication, the group marveled at Donna's ability to confront issues about herself, explore the possible causes, and work out a resolution. For example, Donna's anxiety regarding job interviews had been traced to her desire for approval from her father that had seldom been forthcoming. In the group, Donna worked on dealing with the father in her head. In real life she scheduled a weekend trip to talk with her father about why his approval had been so reluctantly given. At the same time, she scheduled several "throw-away" interviews with firms she would probably not want to work for to practice disassociating her father from the interviewers.

When Donna received the job offer she wanted most, the group openly celebrated her success. Both Donna and, to some extent, the group had been rewarded for their efforts and deserved to enjoy their potency. The group's recognition of Donna's success at working through her feelings and changing her behavior was coupled with sadness over her impending termination from the group. Donna would be in the group for 2 more months before moving from the area to begin her new job.

The group used portions of the eight remaining sessions to help Donna and themselves prepare for her move. All members dealt with their joy and sadness over the loss of an important and successful group member. As Donna worked on her scared feelings about relocating, the other group members acknowledged some of their own fears about eventually having to leave the group and make it on their own. Donna was given the name of a good therapist whom she could contact in her new location and received assistance from the group in identifying issues for further treatment. Because of the successful nature of her work in the group and the ample number of sessions available to deal with her leaving, Donna's termination was a significant growth experience for her and the entire group. Even after she was gone, the group referred to Donna's group experience as an example of individual success within the group.

When Michael left the group 6 months later, the experience was entirely different. Michael had been reluctant to participate in a group form of treatment from the outset. After nearly a year of individual treatment, he and the therapist agreed that he was ready to transfer into the group. Because of Michael's social isolation and insistence that he was the only one who ever felt so lonely and inadequate, both client and therapist saw the group as an excellent treatment vehicle. Despite this intellectual acceptance of the group, Michael did not share the therapist's enthusiasm that he use the group for actively working on his problems.

Michael's 1-year stay in the group was marked by periods of frightened withdrawal and sarcastic rebuffs as the other members attempted to make contact. Several times the group expressed their frustration and anger at the minimal responses they received from Michael compared to the energy they were expending. Generally speaking, however, they reflected the patient, caring attitude of the therapist in accepting the measured sharing and cautious movement that Michael demonstrated. Michael was making some feeling and behavioral changes that he occasionally shared with the group, and the group seemed to accept him as a deviant from the norms as long as he worked toward the treatment goals of the group.

Michael's termination from the group was prompted by a period of moderate improvement during which he was confronted with the possibility of making some definite changes in his depressed and isolated position in life. During one session he raised the possibility that he was getting nothing from the group and wanted to terminate treatment. The group and the therapist pointed out the progress Michael was making and attempted to explore the fear of changing that had prompted his proposed retreat. The group appeared to have some impact and Michael agreed to stay and work on his problems. What was not clear at the time was that Michael attributed his staying to group pressure. He had still not made an autonomous decision to make use of the treatment group.

Ten sessions later Michael did not attend group and the following week a letter arrived announcing his termination. The letter briefly explained how critical Michael felt about the work others were doing in the group and how uncomfortable he felt about sharing his thoughts and feelings with others. The therapist accepted his termination with the reluctant admission that Michael was not willing to make use of the group at that time. The door was left open for Michael to return should he decide to renegotiate a treatment contract at some future time.

The group dealt with Michael's termination very differently than they had with Donna's. Their initial expression of concern over Michael's unwillingness to make major changes was quickly replaced by anger. They thought that they had invested more energy in Michael's treatment than he had and resented the powerless position in which they had been left. Initially they felt guilty about being angry at someone who had been such a "helpless victim" and they backed off from fully expressing their frustration. Since Michael was not there to provide feedback, the group members were left to deal with their fantasies of whether or not they had helped him. Because the therapist had assumed such a caring, accepting position toward Michael's slow progress, the group was hesitant to express their anger at the therapist for "subjecting" them to an unsuccessful member. Several members were fearful that they too might not be helped by the group and that the group would be angry and ask them to leave.

For 6 months following Michael's termination, each of these themes would re-emerge as the group gradually worked through his termination. They were eventually able to resolve what Michael's leaving had meant to each of them personally, to the group collectively, and to the therapist as a symbol of group potency. For many of the group members, Michael's termination provided the opportunity to face important feelings and work them through. They had turned an "unsuccessful" experience into a productive one.

The loss of a group leader is a very significant group event. It is so significant, in fact, that many health care groups are actually planned to terminate when the leader leaves. Groups that have co-leaders are in a better position to absorb the loss of one leader; however, careful planning is required for dealing with this loss. If the group experience has been a positive one, leaders themselves may collude with the group in denying that they are actually leaving. I have been a co-leader in several treatment groups in which the psychiatric resident or student co-leader neglected to tell either me or the group that he was rotating to a different service until just two sessions before he was to leave. This is a powerful example of even therapists' abilities to deny the reality of painful events.

Most therapist terminations are of a relatively planned nature. Students know when their semester is over well ahead of their actual leaving. Very few health professionals change jobs so abruptly that their termination with the group cannot be carefully planned. In some settings a new leader for the group is readily available. For example, in some aftercare clinics the clients and staff have built the reality of student and staff turnover into their treatment structure and clients are accustomed to working with a number of helping people.

In other settings, the nurse who is responsible for a health care group may be the only person qualified or invested in maintaining such a group. When the nurse leaves, there may be no one else to assume responsibility for the group and plans must be made for the members to receive help elsewhere. Regardless of the type of termination—whether member, leader, or group—certain principles apply to dealing with the situation. The role of the leader will be presented as it relates to these termination responsibilities.

Preparation for termination is a process that begins the moment the group leader and potential client make contact. Depending on the type of health care group under consideration, the client will know more or less specifically when termination will occur. If there is a specific contract for behavioral change, the group experience will be over when the desired changes have occurred. When a behavior change group has a plan for maintaining the new behavior, this should be made clear during the client's preparation for entering the group. For example, an outpatient group for hypertensive patients may expect clients to attend group once a month for 6 months once their blood pressure is under control. Clients who require additional assistance following this period can then renegotiate a contract for group attendance that meets their specific needs. This is occasionally true of inpatient groups that allow continued group attendance on an individual basis even after the client has been discharged. Generally speaking, however, the client's participation in the group is over when they return home. In these instances, discharge from the facility is the criteria for leaving the group and should be made clear during the initial interview.

There are also groups, such as natural childbirth classes or classes for diabetic patients, that only meet a specified number of sessions. Some support or socialization groups may have a completely open-ended life span with members free to leave the group when they and the leader agree. The point here is not to cover all possible types of groups, but rather to demonstrate the significance of discussing termination when the client begins a group experience. Most work within health care groups is done with a target for completion—be that defined by time, behavior, or circumstances. It is the leader's responsibility to select clients who are able to work within this context and to share with them the reality of their termination from the group from the initial preparation on. All work that is done within the group can then be planned to safely fit within the allotted time for the individual's participation in the group. For example, a client should not tackle a problem that will take twelve sessions to solve if the group is to meet only two more sessions.

Working through the process of termination is not an easy task for groups to accomplish. Since many people, including group leaders, deny the reality of impending termination, the tendency within health care groups will usually be in the direction of not adequately dealing with the issue. Some clients will "forget" that they are leaving so soon. Others will simply not show up for group and when contacted by the leader will explain why they decided to quit. Still others will write letters of good-bye rather than share their feelings directly with the group.

On the other side of the ledger are clients who go to great lengths not to terminate. Some will continue to generate problems on which to work. Others will experience a sudden return of symptoms just prior to leaving in a valiant attempt to remain in the group. Still others will mentally deny that for them the group is ending. They may arrange to meet with the group members socially and avoid saying good-bye to the group because, "I'll be seeing all of you during the next few weeks anyway."

Working through the process of termination involves activities similar to the working through of other group issues. The issue must be identified and acknowledged, alternative solutions identified and pursued, feelings expressed and dealt with, and a facilitating resolution achieved.

Until more specific data is collected regarding termination in health care groups, the clinician dealing with group and individual issues surrounding termination should use the framework developed by Kubler-Ross[1] to explain the process of death and dying. Dr. Kubler-Ross describes a process in which the dying person moves through several phases that include denial that they are terminally ill, anger over the situation in which they find themselves, bargaining for what they perceive to be more desirable conditions, depression over their impending losses, and acceptance of their existence and mortality.

Drawing on this description of the death and dying process, the group leader can begin to anticipate a variety of phenomena in the group that is anticipating either a group or an individual termination. Individual members will be dealing with the impending loss with a series of feelings—anger, sadness, joy, or fear—or they may be denying the termination entirely. At times all members may share a common experience, such as sadness or denial. There may also be a great deal of individual variation in how members are dealing with the termination and therefore no uniform group feeling will emerge. Most groups will need a great deal of assistance from the leader in working through issues regarding termination.

First, health care groups must be helped to admit and accept the reality of an individual or group termination. In more dependent groups, this first step may consume the majority of the leader's time and attention. I know of one disturbed children's group in which the children persisted through the final session in their belief that they would continue meeting despite repeated information to the contrary. All the grief work with these children regarding their loss of the group had to be done after the fact of termination had been internalized, and this was several weeks after the last group session.

Second, alternative solutions to termination problems need to be identified or pursued. In many groups this may resemble the bargaining phase of Kubler-Ross' grieving process. It is during this phase that some clients will return to an old behavior in an attempt to avoid leaving the group. Clients who have not smoked or gone off their diets for months are suddenly smoking and overeating. Some clients may be expressing fears and self-doubts long since solved but resurrected by the fear of functioning without the group.

This problem can usually be handled by sharing information that this is a common occurrence just prior to termination. It does not mean that the person is back where he started. Once this information has been given, members can be helped to plan alternative ways for adjusting without the group. They can be helped to assess what the group has been doing for them and to determine how else they might provide for this outside the group. One such member realized that the group had provided for her, among other things, with a reason for attending to her own behavior at other times during the week. She then arranged to have lunch with a good friend each week and contracted for each of them to discuss their progress with feeling good about themselves.

Time must be provided prior to termination for both clients and leaders to engage in the identification and pursuit of solutions to termination problems. Depending on the length of the group contract and the dependency of the clients, anywhere from two sessions to 2 months may be required. In structured, time-limited learning groups, much less time is usually spent on this phase of termination. The contract for the group has been clear and time limited and should have fostered much less dependency in the clients. On the other hand, an inpatient ward community group may help long-term psychiatric patients prepare for 2 to 3 months for their discharge from the state hospital. During the course of hospitalization and group membership, these persons invariably become dependent on the group and hospital structure for organizing their lives. The group leader should carefully consider the length of time required for individual members and the entire group to identify and solve termination problems in deciding when to begin dealing with termination issues. The group should always be allowed sufficient time to deal with these issues.

Third, the variety of feelings regarding loss of the group and termination need expression and resolution. The most general and basic feeling associated with loss is sadness. Even when clients are happy over the events surrounding termination, their joy is usually accompanied by some sadness. The woman who has graduated from her weight-loss group may be overjoyed at her success and also sad over leaving the support of the group. Feelings may come in combinations or one feeling may follow another as group members deal with their own or the group's termination. Once expressed, fear over being left without the group's assistance may be followed by anger over being abandoned, which may give way to sadness and mourning for the anticipated loss.

Whatever feelings members may experience surrounding termination, they should be shared, expressed, and resolved during the termination process. This is part of the work done in a well functioning group. When members leave prematurely or deny the reality of termination or their own feelings, their work in the group is unfinished. The group will usually express an uneasy sense of being incomplete when this happens. When group members do express their feelings regarding each other, the leader, and the group experience, they often complete any unfinished business. I remember one support group in which the members took turns sharing all their previously unexpressed feelings toward each other as part of the termination process. The members received more supportive and useful feedback regarding their impact on others during the last three sessions than they had during the previous 3 months. The leader of this group felt it was important that the members finish their business with each other within the group and not carry unexpressed thoughts and feelings away from the experience.

Evaluation of progress for individual members and the group as a whole can be used to facilitate the termination process. Not only is termination a good time to review progress and evaluate the usefulness of the group experience, but engaging in this type of evaluation also appears to facilitate the group's dealing with termination issues. When an individual member is leaving the group, the members may engage in a positive form of reminiscing that underscores the person's progress. Comments such as the following are common: "I'll never forget how angry you looked the first night of group. I thought you weren't even going to stay. It's certainly impressive how much you've changed into an open, caring person. I feel safe with you now." "You're thinking so much better now about how to take care of yourself and not be scared."

When the entire group is ending, the members and leader often reminisce about meaningful events they have shared. "Remember the day we were all angry at Joe for not working as hard as we were to solve his problems. And nobody knew everyone else was angry too until quiet Ruth sneezed and said, 'Oh, shit.' Then we all became aware of how angry we really were and could help Joe see what he had set up." Sad, happy, fearful, and angry times when group members shared a common experience may stand out as significant. These events may be fondly recounted and evaluated by the members.

The group leader can enhance this termination evaluation by directly asking for feedback. What did you like about the way the group was set up? How would you evaluate our work together? Are there things you would have liked changed? What would you suggest we do differently in future groups like this one? In this way members can be assisted to focus on any unfinished business they have with the group leader as well as provide valuable feedback for future use.

It is important also that the leaders share their perceptions of group functioning during this process. Leaders and members alike need validation of their own perceptions. Both the process and the outcomes of the health care group can be examined to provide a feeling of completeness and closure to the group experience.

Planning for the future is an important aspect of evaluating the progress of group members. As members review what they have gotten from the group and what, if anything, they still need from the group, they must plan for alternative ways of meeting their needs once the group has terminated.

Very often the group has provided a supportive environment in which to change and then maintain new behaviors. Members look forward to the group sessions as a time for receiving assistance and positive feedback on their progress. When the group is ending or their experience in the group is over, they will need to plan to receive assistance or positive feedback from others in their environment. Most clients can figure out how to accomplish this once the need is identified and acknowledged as important. When members can write their own termination plan, it is usually a sign that they are ready to leave the group.

Sometimes members will need to leave the group before they are ready. If the group is ending or the person is moving to a new location, it is the leader's responsibility to assist the client in locating an appropriate health care structure for continuing their work. If the client is willing, direct referral to a new group or health care provider is desirable. It is important that all clients, whether they have successfully completed their work in the group or not, know how to find assistance should they need it. The door to continued health care should be left open, and the path for returning should be clear.

In summary, the termination process is an extremely important phase in the life of health care groups. When this phase is given appropriate attention, the group will enjoy the experience of having completed its work. During this phase the leader's functions are to provide a high level of caring and meaning attribution with a concomitant decrease in the stimulation of new issues. The group members must be helped to place their experience together into the larger context of the lives they live outside the group. They take with them new learnings, feelings, and behaviors that they must use without the ongoing support of the group. Hopefully, they will carry their group memory with them as a positive experience from which they have benefitted.

REFERENCE

1. Kubler-Ross, E.: On death and dying, New York, 1969, Macmillan Inc.

Section IV
Evaluation— small group outcomes

Good clinicians evaluate their practice. Excellent clinicians incorporate the feedback of others and their own perceptions of their effectiveness into an ongoing process of evaluation and change. Clinical researchers systematically collect data about their practice that allow them to accurately describe what is occurring, make statements regarding the association of events, or make statements about cause and effect that are generalizable to other clinical settings and generate new knowledge. Both clinical evaluation and clinical research are important to the ongoing improvement of practice and each will be discussed in this section.

Chapter 10 discusses the questions, "What did the group accomplish?" "Was the group effective?" and "What goals and objectives were met in the group?" From a clinical perspective, the answers to these questions are crucial for the continued improvement of the practice. Special emphasis is given to the types of evaluation information to be collected, methods of obtaining evaluative feedback, and the possibilities for interpreting evaluation information. Chapter 10 discusses clinical evaluation.

Chapter 11 assumes a clinical research perspective. Many of the unanswered questions regarding group objectives, structure, process, and outcomes are raised and discussed. Special emphasis is placed on the developmental nature of clinical research of the group variables that operate within health care groups. Chapter 11 discusses clinical research.

Both clinical evaluation and clinical research add an important element to the study of group process. Fig. 3 demonstrates the manner in which the

135

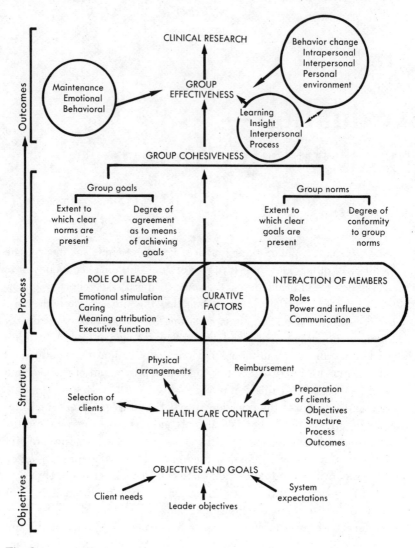

Fig. 3
Model of small group variables—objectives, structure, process, and outcomes (adapted from a model by M. Loomis and J. Dodenhoff, 1970).

effectiveness of the group is a result of the decisions that are made about group objectives, structure, and process. Clinical evaluation provides the group leader with feedback regarding the effectiveness of the health care group or some aspect of the group's structure or process. Very often this feedback is subjective—based on the opinions and observations of the group leader and group members. Feedback and clinical evaluation may be part of the ongoing process of the group in such a way that the leader and members are able to make adjustments and improvements while the group continues to work. The main shortcoming of clinical evaluation is that it does not allow the clinician to make definite statements about *what* worked and *why* it worked. If someone's behavior changed while he was a group member, clinical evaluation will supply that information, but will not allow the conclusion that the group experience was responsible for the change.

Clinical research, on the other hand, is designed in such a manner as to allow for more definitive statements regarding whether someone changed more than he would have had he not been in a health care group. A study that is designed and controlled appropriately can even shed light on *why* and *how* the change occurred. The preceding chapters have posed unanswered questions and researchable hypotheses. It is now time to begin sorting out what we do and do not know about the structure, process, and outcomes of health care groups. Such exploration should eventually contribute to the growing body of clinical nursing knowledge.

10 □ Effectiveness of the group

Good clinicians evaluate the effectiveness of their practice. Whether intuitively or systematically, good clinicians have developed methods for judging the effectiveness of their therapeutic interventions and are constantly adjusting their practice based on observations of their effect on clients. In areas of practice where there are no proven or right ways of doing things, nurses may develop their work with clients in an evolutionary, trial-and-error manner. They hopefully learn from experience what are more or less effective ways of dealing with certain problems. Many areas of nursing currently operate on the basis of trial-and-error because they lack an empirically based body of knowledge from which to practice. While there is certainly room for intuition in a discipline so intimately associated with the health care of human beings, intuitions and insights about what to do in certain situations are no substitute for information gathered in a more systematic fashion.

Nurses who work with clients in health care groups have a very small empirical base from which to operate. As indicated earlier in this text, there are very few right or wrong techniques for working with groups (aside from basic ethical and legal considerations). The group dynamics and group psychotherapy literature can be of some use, but it cannot provide definitive answers regarding the process and outcomes of health care groups. Therefore the nurses who lead such groups must be keenly aware of the need to examine the effectiveness of their group interventions.

138

CLINICAL EVALUATION

Clinical evaluation usually begins with some question. Am I really helping people? What are the things my clients like best about the group? Do they have any suggestions for changes in the group? Do the other professionals in my agency notice any differences in the clients as a result of the group? Are the group members changing? Are the changes generalizing to their lives outside the group? Are the changes maintained over time? Do the clients perceive benefits from the group other than the stated group objectives?

The key to obtaining good evaluative input lies in asking the right questions. That is, nurses who are leading health care groups should be precise in asking the questions to which they are really seeking answers. They may want to know whether or not the group is having a specific desired effect. That implies a yes/no question. They may want to know to what degree certain interventions are effective for the various group members. That necessitates a rating system that allows for a range of responses. They may want to know how one element of the group, for example, the number of members, affects another element, such as satisfaction with the group. That implies a question that will get at the relationship between two variables. They may want to know why something is happening in the group, for example, why attendance is down or why the activity level is up. Or they may want to know what group members consider to be the most significant incidents for them during their time in the group. An answer to this question requires an opportunity to describe experiences in the group, either verbally or in writing.

If the questions are clear, they will lead to the methods the nurse can use to obtain the answers. Basically, there are five sources of information for evaluating the effectiveness of the group: individual group members, the group leader, remaining group members, persons in the members' living environment, and an external supervisor or group expert. Each source provides a certain type of information that answers different questions.

Individual *group members* provide a very personal and subjective type of information. They alone can tell the leader how they feel about their group experience, what they consider to be the most valuable events in the group, and what they need that has not been provided in the group. The group members provide a type of consumer interest survey regarding the effectiveness of the group.

Information can be obtained from group members in a variety of ways.

Some group leaders prefer to periodically ask for input from members regarding the effectiveness of the group. This feedback technique can be built into the ongoing work of the group. The leader should ask questions such as the following: "How do you feel about the way we are working together?" "Is there anything you want from the group that you're not getting?" "What do you want to discuss next week?"

Other group leaders have built in a mechanism for obtaining feedback when members terminate or at the end of the group in the form of a personal interview or questionnaire. Generally, termination questions are designed to discover what was most and least helpful about the group experience and whether or not members have changed as a result of group participation. Occasionally a group leader will make a follow-up contact 3 to 6 months after termination to see if the behavior change has been maintained. There is also a tendency for members to feel very positive about the group at the time of termination and a more realistic evaluation might be obtained by asking for feedback several months later.

Group leaders themselves have valuable perceptions regarding the effectiveness of the group. As mentioned earlier, the leader often has a sense of when things are going well or poorly in the group and may check out these perceptions with the group. Depending on the leader and member conclusions about why the group is proceeding a certain way, adjustments can be made at the time. This ongoing feedback technique is essential to maintaining a viable, well-functioning group.

The leader is also in a position to record before, during, and after perceptions of how group members are progressing with their work in the group. Because leaders bring a very unique, therapeutic perspective to the evaluation of member progress and group effectiveness, they should verify these perceptions with the individual members as well as with the entire group. It is not uncommon for the leader to be frustrated at the slow movement of a group member who is very pleased with the changes she is making in her life outside the group. A group member may expect to have met specific goals such as obtaining a divorce while the group leader is very pleased that she is more assertive and aware of her feelings. These differences in pacing and objectives between group leaders and members make ongoing evaluation and validation of progress imperative.

Remaining group members can be very helpful in providing validation of differing input from that of the leader. One of the advantages of dealing with health care issues in a group setting is the diversity and multiple perspectives that can be provided by more than one person. The group leader should take advantage of this input when attempting to evaluate the effectiveness of the group.

I led one group in which there was a great deal of confusion and frustration generated each time one of the members would talk about his retarded daughter. The other group members would offer suggestions of how to solve what had become a very unpleasant living situation for Robert and the rest of his family. The retarded girl was entering adolescence and becoming too big to manage as they had done when she was younger, yet the family could not decide what to do. Robert seemed unable to accept suggestions from the group even when he asked for them. When he finally did decide on a course of action, placing the girl in a day-care program, he would somehow mess up the plan or not follow through. The net result was an angry group that accused Robert of not wanting to change.

When the leader asked the group to examine the process that was occurring between the group (including the leader) and Robert, everyone admitted to their anger and frustration. Another member, Ann, pointed out that Robert appeared to be the one who was retarded, not his daughter. From that comment, the group process gradually became clearer. The group's anger at Robert was similar to the anger that Robert felt, but was not admitting, toward his daughter. Ann's comment had helped the group to clarify the way in which Robert had assumed his daughter's role with respect to the group and had been acting out the problem rather than solving it. Once the reason for the group's ineffectiveness became clear, so did the reason for Robert's inability to act and he was able to deal with his anger toward his daughter. He then made the decision to place her in a residential school from which she could visit on holidays and weekends. The group's evaluation of its own ineffectiveness had been crucial in helping Robert to solve his problem.

Persons in the group member's environment also have a unique perspective of the effectiveness of the group. Whether solicited or not, their input should always be respected. Some group leaders actively include spouses, family members, roommates, and/or friends in evaluating the effectiveness of the group. They often have the most accurate information about whether or not the member's participation in a health care group is having any effect on their day-to-day behavior. One weight-loss group with which I am familiar used a monitoring system that required the spouses or roommates of group members to co-sign the member's weekly report of eating behaviors. This meant that the significant person in the group member's natural environment had to become familiar with the plan for weight loss and participate in monitoring the change. Often group members would return with valuable suggestions from those in their environments for alterations in their treatment plans. In this way it was useful to include outside persons in evaluating the effectiveness of the group.

It is important to both acknowledge and consider the significant persons in the group member's natural environment. Group members are with the group and leader a relatively small portion of the week. Any changes in their life-style will need to be understood and supported by people with whom they have more frequent contact. These outside persons can also provide significant information as to whether or not change is generalizing from the group environment to the real world in which the group member must function.

Finally, an *external supervisor or group expert* can and should be used to provide the group leader with information regarding the effectiveness of the group. Even the most experienced group leaders should have access to and make use of regular supervision. Some group leaders tape their group sessions, others keep detailed process recordings, and some have an outside observer sit in on a group session periodically. Whatever method of obtaining expert evaluation is used the input is invaluable in improving the leader's abilities and the overall effectiveness of the group. In settings where an "expert" is not available, a professional colleague with knowledge of groups can often provide a fresh perspective and new insights for the leader.

The group leader must be cognizant of the uses that can be made of evaluative feedback. At best they are an external check on the leader's internal perceptions and cognitive understanding of group theory. At the very least they are the result of individual perceptions that cannot be generalized. Consider the frustration of the group leader who decreases the length of the group sessions based on feedback from one group of expectant parents only to find that the next group would like more time to discuss their concerns about taking on the responsibilities of raising a family. Multiple sources of input are essential in deciding about group process changes.

There are times when the feedback of individual group members or the group as a whole must be placed in the context of the treatment that is occurring. Members who want to lose weight quickly with little personal effort may complain that the group is not helping them. A group whose members are supporting each other in not changing may shower the leader with compliments for how good they are feeling. The husband of a woman who is becoming more assertive may provide negative feedback when asked about the benefits of her consciousness-raising group. A clinical supervisor who assumes an active leadership role may become impatient with the nurse who allows for more group participation in problem solving. Evaluation of the group's effectiveness should be based on multiple sources of input carefully interpreted by the group leader. Changes in the health care group should be made cautiously after a variety of types of evidence has been weighed.

GROUP OUTCOMES

While many group leaders are interested in obtaining information about the process that occurs while the group is working together, the primary measure of the effectiveness of the health care group is its outcomes. Has the group accomplished its objectives? Has the group accomplished more than its objectives? Are group members different than when they entered the group?

The outcomes of health care groups can be categorized as maintenance, learning, and/or behavior change. In some groups and for certain group members all three outcomes are appropriate. For example, a group for chronically ill adolescents may have the objectives of maintaining the members' pre-illness level of functioning, teaching the youngsters about their physical limitations, and facilitating the practice of appropriate health care activities. The outcomes of such a group will be measured in terms of the original maintenance, learning, and behavior change objectives.

I prefer to measure group outcomes based on the original goals and objectives of the group. This evaluation of effectiveness can be stated as, "Here is what I intended to do; did I accomplish it?" By the same token, a health care group is a multifaceted form of intervention that may very well have effects well beyond those originally intended. This awareness should prompt the group leader to ask, "What else was accomplished in the group?" What is therefore being proposed is a clinical evaluation that is specific enough to measure the original expected outcomes and general enough to obtain information about unexpected outcomes. For the sake of this discussion each of the three general categories of group outcomes will be presented separately. The reader should be aware that health care groups may accomplish more or different objectives than those originally formulated. Evaluation of group effectiveness should take multiple outcome possibilities into consideration.

Maintenance of emotional and behavioral functioning is one outcome of aprticipation in health care groups. Many preventive groups have the maintenance of functional abilities as their primary objective. Aftercare groups are designed to prevent rehospitalization and maintain their members in the community. Groups for ex-addicts or ex-alcoholics intend to maintain drug- or alcohol-free behavior and prevent readdiction.

Other groups whose primary objective is change and not maintenance advocate the maintenance of functional abilities as a secondary objective. The maintenance of age-appropriate functional abilities is an objective that should always be in the back of the nurse's mind when leading health care groups. For example, a group of young adult patients with multiple sclerosis must learn to care for themselves and adjust their lives to handle the remissions and exacerbations of their illness. They must make these adjustments, however, in light of the personal, professional, and family functioning they wish to maintain. It is not useful for them to give up their functional adult roles and assume a totally dependent sick role. The goal of the group is to help the members arrive at a reasonable life-style that allows them to live in an age- and role-appropriate manner, yet takes their physical limitations and health care needs into consideration.

The evaluation of maintenance goals requires knowledge of normal growth and development as well as the collection of historical and behavioral baseline information about each client. The nurse must be knowledgeable about the developmental tasks that are usually being accomplished at certain ages. The nurse must also collect information about the past and present functional abilities of the group members. What are the appropriate responses present within each member's behavioral repertoire that should be maintained?

This inventory will contain information that may be therapeutically useful as well as an indication of each member's level of functioning. For example, a 35-year-old mother of four youngsters under 8 years of age was referred to a group for child-abusing parents. During the intake interview, the nurse who led the group obtained information about this woman's previous level of personal, professional, and family functioning. She wanted very much to be a good wife and mother, yet had lacked adequate models for these roles during her own childhood. As an adolescent she was often on her own, did well in school, and worked her way into a successful position as a court stenographer. Despite her ability to organize and manage a family and career, she felt she should stay home and become a full-time mother following the birth of her second child. Her husband did not understand her angry outbursts during which she would physically abuse the children, but he seemed committed to helping her change.

What emerged from this intake information was a picture of a woman who had been able to make it on her own professionally, but was lacking sufficient information and experience to assume a healthy role as wife and mother. Not only did her professional capabilities need to be maintained, but these strengths provided a useful intervention strategy for easing the impact of being a mother for four demanding youngsters. The group helped this woman to devise and implement a plan whereby she was able to return to her career on a part-time basis and use a portion of her salary to pay for a housekeeper/babysitter. Once the constant pressures of motherhood were removed, she was in a much better position to take in information about parenting and deal with her own feelings about having been emotionally abandoned by her mother. Maintaining her functional abilities was part of the treatment plan as well as one of the outcomes of this woman's group experience.

Baseline information about members' pre-group levels of emotional and behavioral functioning provides an essential point of comparison in evaluating the effectiveness of the group. To some extent each member becomes his or her own norm for measuring maintenance and progress. Some group members may never be "cured," but are they maintaining their ability to function in their small world? Depending on the age and degree of chronicity of members with limiting physical and emotional problems, the goal of maintenance may be a reasonable one. A clinical specialist who conducted a group for outpatients with chronic obstructive pulmonary disease set goals with each member for the maintenance of their intake levels of respiratory functioning and exercise tolerance. This meant that the group members needed to adjust their lives to the limitations of their illness, while maintaining an active treatment regimen that would prevent further decline in their respiratory status. The group leader and members needed to acknowledge the importance of maintenance goals, and maintenance became the primary measure of the effectiveness of the group.

Learning is another outcome of participation in health care groups. Learning in this context refers to the acquisition of information. This process is primarily cognitive and may or may not lead to behavioral change. Many health care groups established by nurses have learning objectives. Patients need to learn about such things as diets to control their diabetes, the techniques of natural childbirth, how to care for a retarded youngster, how to live with their chronic illness, or how to cope with the death of a family member. There are literally hundreds of such health care learning objectives that can be met in a group.

The most common form of evaluating the outcomes of learning objectives is to administer a pretest and a posttest to determine how much the group members have learned of what was taught. If the acquisition of cognitive information were the only goal of the group, such a test would be an adequate measure of outcomes. However, if the goal is the acquisition of cognitive information, a programmed instruction booklet or videotape cassette, as opposed to a discussion group, might be a more efficient means of delivering the desired information. What usually occurs is that the nurse who established a group to deal with a specific health care topic has objectives for the group that go beyond the acquisition of factual information about a health care issue.

Members who participate in health care groups often learn much more than the facts about a specific health care issue or problem. They learn something about themselves, about how they relate to other people, and about how to change themselves, their relationships, and their personal environment. The process that occurs within a health care group can provide multiple learnings that increase the effectiveness of the group. The reader is reminded of the eleven group process, or "curative," factors discussed in Chapter 3. Each of these factors provides for a unique type of learning within the group setting.

Insight about oneself can be a precursor to behavioral change for some people. This type of intrapersonal learning—learning about one's motivations and how one has arrived at an existential life position—seems to occur more readily in a group setting. Perhaps the experience of altruism and universality that occurs when members are sharing and working on common problems allows the members to see themselves in other people. In accepting and learning about other people, members come to understand and accept themselves.

"My problem is exactly like what Ruth just described," is a commonly heard statement of insight within health care groups. The member will then go on to describe what he has just learned about himself. There may be no immediate evidence of behavioral change, merely the addition of one small piece of self-understanding. This insight, coupled with other awarenesses, may eventually provide the matrix of understanding that can produce change.

The evaluation of group effectiveness should attempt to determine the personal insights members have gained through their group experience. This information is often available at the time the insight occurs and is shared with the group. Thorough process recordings of the group sessions should provide the nurse with an accurate account of member insights. If this information is collected when the group or members are terminating, it may very well lose some of its specificity because specific insights will tend to merge into general statements of self-awareness.

Interpersonal learnings are readily available in a group setting. When the group leader establishes a safe, open, and caring atmosphere, the group members will share their perceptions of each other. Members can learn how they are perceived by others and how they set up certain types of interpersonal relationships. For example, Marge asked the group to help her understand why she was having difficulty in asserting herself at work and why nobody seemed to listen to her. The other group members were able to cite examples of the ways in which Marge had undercut herself when asking for help in the group. The way Marge asked for things made it clear that she did not expect to be heard or to receive what she was requesting. The group members described what they saw Marge doing and the effect it had on them. Marge was then able to utilize the group as a safe place in which to practice and develop more assertive ways of getting her needs met.

The type of interpersonal learning that occurred in Marge's situation can best be evaluated at the time through thorough process recordings and periodic feedback from the group members. The more time that elapses between the event and its recording, the less accurate will be the group's recall of the details and their significance.

The final type of learning that occurs in a health care group involves learning about how to change. This is perhaps the most difficult learning to evaluate since group members and leaders are not likely to know when or how it occurred. They are simply aware at some point that it has occurred. Group members learn to think of themselves differently, to approach their relationships with other people from a new perspective, and to take a more active role in interacting with their environments. Their group experience has modeled for them a new approach to relationships and problem solving that they have gradually assimilated. They have incorporated the process as well as the content of what has gone on in the group and both are available for their continued use.

Group members may be more aware of their own feelings, more open to feedback from others, or more understanding of the time required to change. They may communicate more clearly with their families, be more assertive about getting their needs met, or be less critical of other people. They may think through the options before acting, may respond more spontaneously to other people, or accept that they are less than perfect. They may like themselves better, be more tolerant of others' weaknesses, or respond more calmly to crisis situations. Whatever the difference, they have learned a new process for handling themselves, others, and their environments.

In attempting to evaluate the effectiveness of the group, the nurse may ask some general, open-ended questions. Have you noticed any differences in how you feel about yourself? Are there any differences in your relationships with significant people in your life? Do you feel more or less in control of important events in your life? At times group members may share these process learnings with the group spontaneously: "There I was in this scary situation saying just what Maxine always says about taking time to think." At other times the leader or other group members may become aware that someone is dealing with problems differently. More often than not members participate in and even leave the group without full awareness of what they have learned from their group experience.

Behavior change is the most readily observed and measured of the group intervention outcomes. As stated earlier, behavior either changes or it does not. But most clinicians know it is not quite that simple. Human beings do not always change in a straight line, cause-and-effect manner. And there are still times, despite our increasing knowledge about human behavior, when neither the client nor the health care professional can say for sure why a change has occurred.

It is important, however, that the nurse document and attempt to explain the changes that take place within the health care group. A behavioral baseline and clearly stated behavioral change objectives for clients entering a health care group will greatly assist the nurse in recognizing the incidence and degree of change. In groups that have a specific physiological or physical objective, this statement of baseline and target behaviors is greatly simplified. For example, in a group of hypertensive clients each member can record their entering blood pressure and set a realistic goal for decrease and then maintenance of a lower diastolic and systolic pressure to be achieved in a certain period. The same is true of a weight-loss group, with number of pounds being the target behavior. Once the final blood pressure or weight goal has been negotiated, smaller goals for each week can be established. Initially clients in a weight-loss group may contract to observe and record their eating behaviors. They may then begin to alter these eating behaviors in an agreed-upon manner and any actual weight loss may only begin occurring once these initial changes are in effect. Each weekly contract requires small behavioral changes that will lead to an eventual change of larger magnitude. These sequential changes are each important for the nurse and the group members to note. The reader is referred to the techniques for utilizing a behavioral nursing process outlined by Loomis and Horsley.[1] Their model, based on the principles of operant conditioning, is useful whenever there is a specific behavioral change contract within a health care group.

There are many changes that members accomplish within a health care group that cannot be categorized as physical or physiological. A group of adolescent boys may learn to compete in a socially acceptable manner through the use of games and athletics. A group of college women may develop new strategies for combining a career and a family. A group of patients about to be discharged from a psychiatric hospital may acquire a personal acceptance of their emotional problems and increase their ability to explain their problems to family members, friends, and employers. A group of women with mastectomies may learn to accept their own bodies by working with other women about to undergo a similar procedure. The behavioral changes observed in these groups are of an intrapersonal, interpersonal, and personal environmental nature.

As people deal with their problems in a health care group, they gradually come to the point of dealing differently with themselves. Some group members have described a greater acceptance of their own strengths and weaknesses, not putting themselves down for who they are or what they are doing, and feeling more comfortable with themselves. After sharing hidden parts of themselves in a group, they are much more willing to offer themselves the same acceptance they experienced from the group members. They no longer need to deny a part of their being to themselves or the outside world.

One measure of the effectiveness of the health care group is the new decisions that members make about themselves. Examples of such decisions include the businessman who decided to stop overworking himself, the woman who decided to be close to people and make new friends rather than hiding her isolation in an alcoholic stupor, and the adolescent who decided that it was okay to be an engineer rather than a football player following the amputation of his leg. The nurse who assists group members in arriving at new decisions about themselves should be sensitive to their importance as an index of personal change accomplished within the health care group.

What often happens is that once people feel differently about themselves, they begin to relate to others differently. Group members will usually report significant changes in their personal and professional relationships following a change in how they relate to themselves. Other group members and those in the person's natural environment will notice that something is different. The businessman who decided to stop overworking will begin to turn down extra assignments at the office and spend more time with his family. The woman who decided to be close to people will leave the isolation of her home and plan activities where she can make new friends. The adolescent who has formulated a new life plan will stop being angry and closed with his family and begin to share his goals with them.

Depending on the degree of acceptance of a given change in the group member's natural environment, the change may be met with varying degrees of reinforcement. The businessman's boss will probably not appreciate the idea of the man's turning down work. The housewife's family may have some concerns about her not being home all the time when they feel they need her. Very often the group member's new interpersonal behavior will need some time to become stabilized and supported by those around them. This fact is important to recognize when attempting to evaluate the effectiveness of changes made within the health care group.

Eventually, group members who have changed how they feel about themselves and how they relate to others will also demonstrate increased ability in dealing with their personal environment. They will know what they want, how to communicate with others about it, and how to develop a plan for getting their needs met. Often group members will discuss their plans with the group before attempting to implement them in the real world. For example, the businessman needs to develop strategies for decreasing his workload without losing his job. He may eventually decide that decreasing his workload will not be tolerated in his current position and that he will need to change jobs. His decision may eventually require that he find and/or cultivate an environment that will work for him. This type of mastery over one's personal environment is often evidence of the effectiveness of the health care group.

While there is no guarantee that the learning that occurs in a health care group will result in behavioral change, there does appear to be some connection between the two. Some clients enter a health care group ready to change and only require information about how to accomplish their desired goals. Other clients enter a health care group uncomfortable about some aspects of their lives, take in the available information, and persist in remaining uncomfortable. It is sometimes difficult to know what clients have done with the information they received and the learnings that took place within the group. The timing of change is different for different people. Some people will change immediately and not understand why until later, while others will know all of the whys and not change until months later.

Because of the above phenomena and the lack of a totally controlled environment in which change can be attributed directly to the member's participation in a health care group, there is a difference between clinical evaluation and clinical research regarding group effectiveness. Clinical evaluation allows the nurse to determine whether or not the group members have changed. This is important clinical information to systematically collect. The goals of the health care group should influence the maintenance, learning, and behavioral change data collected.

The answers to why and how group members have changed will need to be sought through clinical research of health care groups. Strategies for answering these questions are discussed in Chapter 11.

REFERENCE

1. Loomis, M. E., and Horsley, J. A.: Interpersonal change: A behavioral approach to nursing practice, New York, 1974, McGraw-Hill Book Co.

11 □ Group process—research questions

This chapter is designed to raise far more questions than it answers. To some this approach may be unsettling. Most clinicians like to think they know what they are doing and why they are doing it. After all, nurses practice day in and day out and a good clinician has somehow figured out what works and how to help clients change.

The fact of the matter is that we know very little in any systematic fashion about the process of health care groups. Even if we can document the effectiveness of a certain type of health care group, there is often a difference of opinion or conflicting explanations of why and how the group was effective. Clinical nursing research must be conducted to generate new knowledge about the functioning of health care groups.

Many unanswered questions will be raised in this chapter. These questions will be focused on the objectives, structure, process, and outcomes of health care groups as discussed in the preceding ten chapters. While some attention will be given to what to measure, how to measure, and when to measure certain group variables, this is not intended to be a discussion of research methodology and data analysis techniques. There are other texts available that more adequately address these topics. Rather, it is my intent to stimulate current and potential nurse researchers to consider a systematic approach to empirically exploring the process of health care groups. In this manner they will begin providing answers to the many unanswered questions.

Throughout this text I have drawn upon the research conducted by the social scientists in the field of group dynamics and that designed to study group psychotherapy. Many of these studies need to be replicated and extended to encompass health care groups before clear assertions can be made about nursing interventions. As this research is conducted, nursing will be developing its own body of knowledge related to its health care function and not merely borrowing knowledge that may or may not apply to nursing practice.

GROUP OBJECTIVES

There is a need for systematic information regarding the client needs and leader objectives that can be met within a health care group and the degree of congruence that must exist between the two for a successful group experience. What will happen if the leader expects the group members to change some aspect of their behavior and the group members simply want to talk about their problems and share common experiences? Are the goals of socialization and behavior change compatible? Or what happens if the needs of only one or two members differ from those of the group and the objectives of the leader? How many divergent types of needs can be met in any one group? How many conflicting sets of objectives can a group manage and does it matter whose objectives they are?

Clinical research of the above and related questions will depend on developing a system for classifying and coding both client needs and therapist objectives. This system will need to be applicable across groups so that comparative data can be obtained. It may be that one type of group, e.g., a resocialization group, is able to tolerate more divergent objectives than some other type, e.g., a learning–behavior change group.

An even more difficult conceptual and measurement problem that touches on almost all aspects of health care group research is the development of outcome criteria and measurement tools. To raise the question of whether or not divergent needs and conflicting objectives can be met in the same group implies that there is some clear method for measuring the outcomes of the health care group experience. These outcomes should in some way be related to, but not restricted to, the original needs of the clients and objectives of the group leader. Lieberman et al[1] used an extensive collection of subjective and objective measures of group effectiveness. They obtained ratings of group effectiveness from the participants themselves, the group leaders, co-participants, and friends or relatives of the participants; they collected this data at the time of the group termination and 6 months later. Since they conceptualized encounter groups as "people-changing groups," they were interested in measures that captured a variety of aspects of intrapersonal and interpersonal change. They attempted to measure changes in values, attitudes, and feelings, as well as overt behavior.

The reader is encouraged to explore a wide variety of outcome criteria in researching health care groups. The original client needs and therapist objectives for the group should assist in conceptualizing and structuring the outcome criteria. However, the wide range of possible outcomes related to the group experience suggests that the researcher remain open to the possibility of unanticipated beneficial and detrimental outcomes. Multiple sources of subjective and objective data will provide the researcher with much information for determining the effectiveness of the group.

There is also a need to explore the impact of system expectations on the functioning and effectiveness of the group. It is conceivable that the presence of certain variables within the agency or program housing the health care group can facilitate its functioning. It is also possible that there are certain organizational factors that are detrimental to the functioning of groups. Knowledge of factors such as the expected roles of various health team members, the treatment philosophy and objectives of the program, the climate for innovation, and the availability of resources (time, materials, space, staff) for health care groups, and their correlation with the effectiveness of certain groups would save potential group leaders many unnecessary hours of frustration. If the researcher could begin to describe and quantify the organizational environment in which a group is most likely to succeed, the leader could work more directly at establishing a favorable organizational milieu before initiating a health care group.

Another area that deserves further exploration is the use of groups in comparison with other forms of health care intervention. What client needs can best be met in a group? Which nurse objectives and health care system expectations are best suited to a group form of intervention? To date these questions have primarily been answered by the preferences of individual health care practitioners. Some clinicians prefer to work with clients in groups. Others prefer individual teaching or counselling. Still others prefer not to talk extensively with their clients at all.

It would be useful to have more systematic data regarding the utility and timing of group health care interventions in dealing with client problems. For example, is a crisis group as effective as individual crisis intervention in assisting people who are experiencing a high level of situational stress? Is the crisis resolved more quickly? Does it stay resolved? Is the level of growth and learning from the crisis enhanced by one form of intervention versus another?

This same series of questions can be raised about any client need ranging from rape counselling to learning a self-care procedure, to intensive psychotherapy. We do not know if clients will lose weight, learn colostomy care, or adjust to a newly diagnosed illness any better if provided with an appropriate health care group. Further, we are lacking crucial data about the correct timing and combination of health care interventions. Do women, experiencing recent alterations in body image and feminine sex role functioning, do better if they receive group support in addition to, or in place of, individual support? How soon postoperatively are they able to make use of the group? Are there certain women who will not benefit from a health care group, and can this be predicted ahead of time?

The effectiveness of groups as compared with other types of interventions must also be looked at in light of the relative efficiency and economy across modes of treatment. Does one intervention take longer or cost more despite its equal effectiveness? What is the length and extent of follow-up required for permanent change? Are there enough clients available at any one time to maintain a viable, functioning group? Are there adequately prepared staff and supervision available? All of these factors can affect the efficiency and economy of certain health care groups and should be considered in the determination of group effectiveness.

GROUP STRUCTURE

The selection of clients for health care groups is a complex issue—one that would certainly benefit from rigorous clinical research. The group psychotherapy research cited in Chapter 4 focuses on specific patients who should be excluded from groups.[2-8] There is general consensus that persons who are brain damaged, suicidal, addicted to drugs or alcohol, acutely psychotic, or sociopathic should be excluded from intensive, outpatient group psychotherapy. Yet, many clinicians have successfully treated such clients in groups. Further, there is no reason to assume that clients excluded from intensive, outpatient group psychotherapy should also be excluded from other types of health care groups.

Research is needed to clarify the characteristics of the client, the preferences or characteristics of the leader, and the factors inherent in the group that interact to produce a successful health care group experience. The group therapy and group dynamics research[9,10] suggest that the member's attraction to the group and his general popularity in the group are the best predictors of successful outcomes. Is this also true of health care group members? Does the preference of the group leader for certain types of clients influence their functioning within the group and the benefits they derive? What factors within the group itself can be used to predict the success of potential group members? Are there good or bad times to introduce a new member into the group? In which groups can turnover of members be tolerated and in which is a stable membership important? Are inclusion rather than exclusion criteria more effective as a means of selecting group members?

There are several hypotheses stated in Chapter 4 that require extensive research across types of health care groups. The first of these is that group members who subscribe to the goals of the group and are capable of and willing to adhere to the norms of the group will be effective, successful group members. What will happen to group members who do not subscribe to the goals of the group? Can a client desirous of behavior change meet his objective in a group whose goal is insight, or can a client who needs support be accommodated in a learning–behavior change group? Is this sharing of common goals more important in some types of groups than others? How much deviance can a group tolerate with respect to its norms? What happens to the group process and individual member functioning when a member is not willing or able to adhere to the group norms? For example, is a client who cannot attend regularly disruptive? Will he benefit from the group? Will a group assist someone with a physical or emotional handicap that interferes with their capability to adhere to group norms? Will they allow the leader to offer special assistance to such a person? What determines whether they are willing to adjust to such deviance?

The second hypothesis relates to the appropriate mix of clients within a health care group. It is hypothesized that the optimum mix of clients can be obtained by selecting group members who are *homogeneous* with respect to their commitment to the group goals and their ability to participate in the group norms and *heterogeneous* with respect to other personal, physical, or emotional characteristics. Leaders of health care groups need to begin describing and quantifying the mix of clients in their groups. This data then needs to be analyzed across many types of health care groups to determine the impact of the mix of clients on the process and outcomes of the group. Only then can the nurse select clients for a health care group in something other than an intuitive manner.

Reimbursement is another group structure variable that requires careful research. Do clients who pay for the services of a health care group make a stronger commitment to utilizing the group and have better outcomes? Are there certain types of clients for whom paying for the group is a more important issue than others? Is the value of reimbursement related to the socioeconomic status of the client? What types of potential clients will refuse to participate in a health care group if a fee is charged? Is a partial fee or exchange of services a useful alternative for clients who indicate they are unable to pay the full fee? Data about the relative utility to the client of charging for health care groups may assist nurses in deciding how to structure the question of reimbursement for their own group practice.

Another group structure variable of some importance is the preparation of clients for the group. Do clients who have received information about the group ahead of time make a smoother entry into the group, participate more readily, and/or receive greater benefits from the group? In their 1966 study, Yalom et al[11] found that clients who had been systematically prepared for their group therapy experience exhibited more faith in therapy and engaged in significantly more group and interpersonal interaction than the nonprepared clients as measured in the second and twelfth sessions. This study needs to be replicated to see whether or not the findings extend to various types of health care groups.

If it is determined that clients do benefit from preparation for participation in health care groups, what should be the structure and content of that preparation? How structured or unstructured should the preparation be? Are written materials, a formal examination by the leader, a meeting with another group member, or an informal question and answer discussion more effective? What are the relative advantages of sharing affective information about what the new client may experience in the group versus sharing more cognitive information about how and why the group functions? Should both affective and cognitive information be shared? A variety of techniques for the preparation of clients needs to be researched and knowledge systematically assembled about the types of clients and groups with which they are most effective.

The final group structure variable in need of research is the health care contract. Does a clear contract between the client, the nurse, and the group facilitate the course of treatment? How specific must the contract be to be effective? How does the health care contract change during the course of group participation? What is the relationship between the client's contract and his outcomes from group participation? Undoubtedly there are many additional questions about the structure of health care groups that will emerge from the clinician's experience. Each clinical question offers an opportunity to add to our small body of knowledge about health care groups and how they can best be structured.

GROUP PROCESS

The ways in which health care groups accomplish their work represents a vast, uncharted territory for the clinical researcher. Much of the available research on group dynamics has been conducted by social and organizational psychologists on populations of college students or in business, industrial, and community settings. It is not clear how generalizable these findings are to health care settings and the types of clients with whom nurses are concerned. Because of the difficulties of conducting research in naturalistic settings, many group process studies have been conducted in laboratory situations with groupings of people who are a group only for the purposes of the study. Since we are not certain of the similarities and differences between laboratory groups and ongoing, working groups in the real world, there is a great need for replication of these studies in the world in which the group lives and functions.

What is the process that occurs within health care groups? Does the theoretical orientation of the leader make a difference? What are the stages through which the group develops? What kind of member interaction can be expected in health care groups? What are the curative factors that are significant at the various stages of the group's life? What is the most effective role for the health care group leader at each of the stages? What is the most effective content/process emphasis for groups having different objectives and clients? What is the function of group cohesiveness in various types of health care groups? These are only a few of the questions to which answers must be sought if we are to add to our knowledge of the process of health care groups.

Leadership style, roles, intervention behaviors, and theoretical orientation appear to have an impact on the process and outcomes of health care groups. Lieberman et al[1] found that how leaders conducted themselves made a substantial difference in the relative benefit or harm experienced by the encounter group participants in their study. Differences in leader behaviors, however, were found to be unrelated to their theoretical orientations. Is this finding also true for different types of health care groups?

Further research is needed to determine whether or not the leader behaviors of stimulation, caring, meaning-attribution, and executive function, which were isolated in the Liberman et al[1] research, are useful categories for examining leadership behaviors in health care groups. If these four behaviors are found to be separate, distinguishable, and inclusive categories, a number of research questions can be raised using these leader functions. What is the most effective blend of these functions for leaders of health care groups? Does the appropriate mixture of these functions vary depending on the client needs, group objectives, or stage of group development? Is there a higher incidence of executive functioning necessary in the early sessions of the group? Is a high proportion of caring and meaning-attribution desirable in all types of health care groups (support, task accomplishment, socialization, learning–behavior change, human relations, and psychotherapy) or only certain ones? Are the findings of Lieberman et al[1] that the most effective leadership style is one of high caring, high meaning-attribution, moderate executive functioning, and moderate stimulation supported across types of health care groups? These and many more questions concerning the role of the leader are amenable to clinical investigation once a system of categorizing and measuring leadership functions in health care groups is developed and standardized.

A similar set of questions can be raised about the process through which health care groups progress in accomplishing their objectives. Is there a predictable, identifiable progression of stages in the development of the group? If so, what is it? Do the concepts of orientation, working, and termination phases have any relevance in describing health care groups? Do Yalom's[12] phases of "In-Out," "Top-Bottom," and "Near-Far" have any relevance in describing health care groups? It may be that a certain group such as a learning–behavior change group does not go through the same progression of stages that a psychotherapy group does. The similarities and differences in group development across types of groups need to be described and quantified.

Once these stages of group development have been clarified, the complex research of group process can begin. What type of member interaction can the leader expect and facilitate at the various stages and in different types of groups? Can the members of a task group be expected to help each other with subtasks during the early meetings of the group? Do members of a learning–behavior change group also learn to care about and support each other? If so, when can this caring be expected to emerge and how can it be fostered? Does the degree of goal specificity influence the group's movement through the stages? What impact does the time frame in which the group is functioning have on the group's development? Are there different developmental stages for long-term versus short-term groups? For open-ended versus time-limited groups?

Finally, what is it about the group that really helps people? Does the role of the leader and the curative factors employed vary across the life of the group? What is the significance of each curative factor in each of the different types of groups? Is group cohesiveness as significant in a task group or learning–behavior change group as it is in a support or psychotherapy group? Is interpersonal learning an important curative factor regardless of the type of group and its objectives? Are there certain curative factors whose presence or absence significantly influence the outcomes of the group experience? Are there curative factors that operate in health care groups that have not as yet been identified in the group dynamics and group psychotherapy literature? If so, their identification and measurement will contribute significantly to our understanding of groups in general and health care groups within nursing practice.

The function of group cohesiveness within various types of health care groups needs to be explored. Cohesiveness has been described as a curative factor—an essential ingredient as well as an outcome of healthy group functioning. This dual use of the concept of cohesiveness presents a dilemma for the clinical researcher since cohesiveness needs to be a dependent and an independent variable simultaneously. What appears to be needed is some more basic, descriptive work on the definition of cohesiveness. What do clinicians mean when they use the term? What are group leaders and members observing and experiencing when they describe a group as cohesive? It is likely that cohesiveness is a general concept that can be broken down into more specific variables, the measurement of which would yield a cohesiveness score or rating.

In Chapter 7 I began developing a model for examining group cohesiveness. It is hypothesized that the extent to which clear goals are present and the degree of agreement as to the means of achieving those goals will influence the development of cohesiveness in health care groups. It is further hypothesized that the extent to which clear norms are present and the degree of conformity to the group norms will influence the development of cohesiveness in health care groups. The interactions among clarity and agreement regarding goals and norms need to be explored. To what extent do these factors influence group cohesiveness? Are there other important factors that influence cohesiveness in health care groups? Is similarity of members a factor that affects cohesiveness, and if so, along what dimensions is similarity measured? What can the group leader do to foster and develop group cohesiveness?

If clarity and agreement with respect to the goals and norms of the group influence the development of group cohesiveness, it is important to isolate the factors that affect goals and norms. I have hypothesized that the group goals are directly related to the time frame in which the group is functioning and the group norms are directly related to the stability of group membership. This means that the goals of the group will vary as a function of the time in which the group has to work as a group, while the norms of the group will vary as a function of how stable the group membership remains. These hypotheses need to be tested across conditions of open and closed membership and groups that have open and closed time frames. What is the impact of unstable membership on the group? What is the interaction between membership turnover and the time in which the group has to accomplish its objectives? Are certain types of group goals and objectives less dependent on stable group membership? What factors other than or in addition to the time frame and stability of membership influence the goals and norms of health care groups?

Within the context of this book, cohesiveness has been regarded as a cause rather than an effect. It has been assumed that a high level of group cohesiveness will have a positive effect on the outcomes of health care groups. Clinical research will need to test the validity of this assumption. There might very well be certain health care groups in which cohesiveness is unrelated to the outcomes of group participation. This entire conceptual area is open to clinical investigation.

In addition to group cohesiveness, there are other group process variables that have a potential impact on the outcomes of health care groups. The process variables of resistance to change, closeness, conflict, working through, and termination are discussed from a clinical perspective in Chapters 8 and 9. I have described these issues and proposed clinical management strategies based on my own clinical experience. There is a need for thorough descriptive research of these group phenomena. To what extent do these process variables occur across different types of health care groups? What effect do they have on the movement of the group toward accomplishing its objectives? What roles can the leader assume in assisting the group to deal with these process issues? What interventions are effective? What is the appropriate content versus process emphasis on health care groups? When is it important to focus on process issues in a task or learning–behavior change group? When is it important to focus on content in a process-oriented group?

Initial research will need to be directed at describing what occurs in different types of health care groups. Once the process variables are more clearly defined, measurement of their incidence and impact on group functioning can be identified. Lastly, the leader interventions that lead to effective resolution and beneficial group outcomes can be tested.

GROUP OUTCOMES

There are several relevant questions that can be raised about the outcomes of health care groups. Did the group have an effect? What was the effect? What caused the effect? In the previous chapter, consideration was given to the clinical evaluation of the maintenance, learning, and behavior change outcomes of health care groups. Suggested sources of evaluative information included the group members themselves, the group leader, co-participants in the group, persons in the group member's living environment, an external supervisor or group expert. It was further proposed that multiple measures of group outcomes be utilized and that there be a strong connection between the original goals and objectives of the group and the group outcomes being evaluated. These same recommendations can be applied, when approaching the task of clinical research, to the outcomes of health care groups.

The primary difference between clinical evaluation and clinical research of group outcomes is in the level of control imposed on the variables being measured. Control is the ability of the researcher to manipulate and measure specific variables. A well-controlled study allows one to clearly state that one variable (group participation) had an impact on another variable (maintenance of weight loss). This is usually accomplished by comparing the outcomes (maintenance of weight loss) of group members with a comparable sample of people who received another form of intervention (regular clinic visits) or no intervention at all. The greater the similarity of these clients on all factors except the form of intervention they are receiving, the greater the experimental control and the stronger the conclusion that the group had or did not have an impact on maintenance of weight loss.

The goal of experimental control is to be able to state clearly that there was an effect and what caused that effect. To make those statements, the researcher must control for the effect of extraneous variables. For example, maybe the people who were placed in the group were different in some way from those who had other forms of treatment. Maybe they would have maintained their weight loss whether or not they had participated in the group. Maybe the group leader is good at getting people to take care of themselves and the group had no impact at all.

There are many ways to design studies and numerous data analysis techniques that are described in research texts. The previous example represents one of many ways to design a controlled study of group outcomes. The point to be made here is that the generation of systematic knowledge about the effects of health care groups depends on the conduct of scientific, controlled clinical studies. If the research is well designed, the conclusions about cause and effect will add to the scientific knowledge in a given field. That is the ultimate goal of research in any field or discipline and nursing is no exception.

Numerous questions about the objectives, structure, process, and outcomes of health care groups have been raised in this chapter. Many of these questions can be asked in the form of (1) What is X?, (2) Does X make a difference?, and (3) Is X more effective than Y? There is a general developmental research process inherent in these questions regardless of the group variable represented by X. This process, described below, is necessary because the clinical research of health care groups is just beginning.

What is X? The clinical researcher must begin by defining the concept or group variable under investigation. For example, what is a health care contract? How is the contract evident in clinical practice? Do the leader and the group members define the contract similarly? What are the components of a health care contract? What is the range of contracts evident in different types of health care groups? Are there some general categories or types of contracts that emerge from the data? The overall goal of this series of questions is to define and describe the clinical concept—in this case the health care contract. One place to begin is to describe specifically what is happening in clinical practice. An alternative starting point would be to sit down and decide what a health care contract *should be* conceptually and then how it *should* manifest itself in clinical practice. The end result of either approach will need to be the operational definition of a concept with specific definitions of its component parts. For example, a health care contract might eventually be defined as "an openly negotiated, clearly stated set of mutual expectations that indicates what the nurse and client can expect of each other with respect to the client's health care." The component parts of the contract may be (1) a set of shared objectives, (2) mutual understanding of the structure and process of health care, and (3) mutually determined outcomes.

The goal of defining X is to clarify the concept and identify variables that represent separate, distinguishable, and inclusive categories that can be measured. Instruments can then be developed that will indicate the presence or absence of X or the amount of X present in any situation. For example, is there a health care contract? What components of a health care contract are present or absent in this situation? Each of the group variables presented in this text must be subjected to this process. These include but are not limited to: client needs, leader objectives, system expectation, group objectives, group structure, curative factors, interaction of members, role of the leader, group cohesiveness, group norms, group goals, group effectiveness, and group outcomes.

Does X make a difference? Finding the answer to this question depends on having clearly defined X as well as having clearly defined some outcome criteria. For example, in asking whether or not having a complete health care contract is correlated with satisfactory or excellent group outcomes, one needs to have defined both "complete health care contract" and "satisfactory or excellent group outcomes." Many of the questions raised earlier in this chapter will require the researcher and clinician to clearly define a set of group outcomes and ways to measure them. I propose the previously described categories of maintenance, learning, and behavior change as a place to begin in defining the outcomes of health care groups.

Is X more effective than Y? To answer this cause and effect question requires a controlled experimental design. Both X and Y must be defined and measurable. Effectiveness must be stated in terms of measurable outcomes. For example, does a complete health care contract produce more stable maintenance of weight loss in health care groups than a system in which the nurse established client goals? In answering this research question, both interventions (mutual contract and nurse goals) must be operationalized and the outcome of stable maintenance of weight loss must be defined. The conduct of experimental research is clearly dependent on the definition, isolation, and measurement of relevant health care group variables. The relationships among these variables then need to be tested before cause and effect studies can be designed.

In summary, it is imperative that the clinician who leads health care groups adopt a questioning stance while engaged in daily practice. We do not know what the right and wrong ways are of structuring and conducting health care groups. We know very little in any systematic fashion about the relative advantages and disadvantages of different health care group interventions. Yet every day we must and do practice. There is a great need for clinicians and researchers to join together in the process of exploring clinical practice in all areas of nursing. The use of health care groups represents one of the exciting, unexplored avenues for clinical investigation and the generation of scientific knowledge.

REFERENCES

1. Lieberman, M. A., Yalom, I. D., and Miles, M. B.: Encounter groups: First facts, New York, 1972, Basic Books.
2. Nash, E., Frank, J., Gliedman, L., Imber, S., and Stone, A.: Some factors related to patients remaining in group psychotherapy, Int. J. Group Psychother. 7:264-275, 1957.
3. Johnson, J. A.: Group psychotherapy: A practical approach, New York, 1963, McGraw-Hill Book Co.

4. Slavson, S. R.: A textbook in analytic group psychotherapy, New York, 1964, International Universities Press.
5. Slavson, S. R.: Criteria for selection and rejection of patients for various kinds of group therapy, Int. J. Group Psychother. **5:**3-30, 1955.
6. Corsini, R., and Lundin, W.: Group psychotherapy in the mid-west, Group Psychother. **8:**316-320, 1955.
7. Rosenbaum, M., and Hartley, E.: A summary review of current practices of ninety-two group therapists, Int. J. Group Psychother. **12:**194-198, 1962.
8. Bach, G.: Intensive group therapy, New York, 1954, Ronald Press.
9. Yalom, I. D., Houts, P. S., Zimerberg, S. M., and Rand, K. H.: Prediction of improvement in group therapy, Arch. Gen. Psychiatry **17:**159-168, 1967.
10. Cartwright, D., and Zander, A., (eds.): Group dynamics, New York, 1968, Harper & Row, Publishers.
11. Yalom, I. D., Houts, P. S., Newell, G., and Rand, K. H.: Preparation of patients for group therapy, Arch. Gen. Psychiatry **17:**416-427, 1967.
12. Yalom, I. D.: The theory and practice of group psychotherapy, New York, 1975, Basic Books.

Index